Contents

LIST OF TABLES

LIST OF FIGURES

ABBREVIATIONS

BOP	Balance of Payments
CDG	Curriculum Development Center
CG	Consultative Group (Paris Club)
CEP	Community Education and Participation
CMMU	Community Management and Monitoring Unit
DAC	Development Assistance Committee (of OECD)
DCO	Development Cooperation Office
DESA	Drought Emergency in Southern Africa
DIMS	Drought Impact Monitoring System
DWA	Department of Water Affairs
EMU	Educational Materials Unit
FINNIDA	Finnish International Development Agency
FAO	Food and Agricultural Organisation
FEMAC	Foreign Exchange Management Committee
GDP	Gross Domestic Product
GNP	Gross National Product
GRZ	Government of the Republic of Zambia
IMF	International Monetary Fund
JICA	Japanese International Cooperation Agency
KKF	Kenneth Kaunda Foundation (now ZEPH)
MEPSU	Ministry of Education Procurement and Supplies Unit
NATCAP	National Cooperation Assessment and Programmes
NCDP	National Commission for Development Planning
NERP	New Economic Recovery Programme
NGO	Non-Governmental Organisation
NORAD	Norwegian Agency for International Development
ODA	Overseas Development Assistance
OECD	Organisation of Economic Cooperation and Development
PAM	Programme Against Malnutrition
PPM	Programme for the Prevention of Malnutrition
SADC	Southern African Development Community
SAP	Structural Adjustment Programme
SASDA	Secretariat for Analysis of Swedish Development Assistance
SIDA	Swedish International Development Authority
UN	United Nations
UNDP	United Nations Development Programme
USAID	United States Agency for International Development
VHK	Government Procurement Office (Finland)

Chapter 1

An Introduction to the Study

THE PROBLEM

There is an increasing concern about the future of aid in Africa. The region has fallen behind the rest of the developing world in virtually all indicators; even worse, the gap between Africa and other regions in the Third World continues to grow. In spite of aid, the countries in Africa have become poorer and poorer. Such a performance has shaken the confidence of both donors and recipients in Africa. Indeed, the effectiveness of aid has been increasingly questioned in the North and a feeling of aid fatigue has set in.

During the last 10 years the effectiveness of aid has become increasingly questioned. The growing aid fatigue depends on two different, but mutually reinforcing, development tendencies. In the donor countries, particularly in Europe, economic growth has been trailing and resources for public sector growth have been more limited than before.

Sweden is a good example of this development. Economic growth has been sluggish, and the economy has actually been stagnating during the late 1980s and 90s. The public sector's share of the national income must be adapted to a lower level of resource availability than what we have been accustomed to during the post-war period. At the same time aid has been a politically uncontroversial subject. There has been a consensus regarding the political goal of allocating 1% of GDP to aid. Aid has during many years expanded at the same pace as the Gross Domestic Product (GDP), something which other parts of the public sector have not been allowed to do. A weak or even negative growth coupled with a fast growing budget deficit has changed this situation. Aid is now facing the same adjustment demands as the rest of the public sector.

Competition within the public sector will become increasingly fierce. Aid will no longer receive the same political protection as before. A major task of aid will therefore be to show that it actually uses its resources in the best possible way. This has not always been an easy task.

Fighting poverty by supporting economic growth and development in the least developed countries has been and continues to be a major objective of aid. Since independence, however, most African countries have gone through a negative, or in the best case a stagnating economic development. Most welfare indicators are pointing in the wrong direction. The poor are getting poorer. Add to this frequent reports about different scandal projects.

No wonder that the credibility of aid has been questioned. Is aid a major cause of this negative development? Or has it prevented an even worse decline in living standards? Or has it simply been without any impact at all? These are questions which aid agencies and host countries alike, have to struggle with and provide convincing answers to.[1]

There have been many studies on aid effectiveness over the years. They differ slightly in how they approach the problem, some provide important insights, others are just replications of what is already known. Where does this modest contribution to the debate on aid effectiveness fit in? In the following section we shall try to position ourselves and define the purpose of this book.

AID EFFECTIVENESS

Africa and its donors seem to have moved into a state of disillusionment, which is particularly dangerous in a decade when many Africans still eke out a subsistence existence. The problem of aid effectiveness has, therefore, come to occupy a central position in the debate on development in Africa.

As it has been more and more difficult to see any positive connection between aid and economic development the question arises: is aid doing the right thing at the right time and in the right way? In the light of growing economic problems among the donor countries, the general public have a right to demand aid which is both effective and efficient. What then does this concept stand for and what do we know about the effectiveness of aid?

Broadly speaking, aid effectiveness is defined for the purpose of this study in terms of both (a) the given project/programme's ability to achieve its set goals and objectives and (b) the degree to which such achievement is sustainable. Sustainability in this respect entails the project's ability, both real and potential, to realise positive benefits through the use of the most cost-effective, yet socially and politically acceptable, means for an extended period that goes beyond the time major financial, managerial and technical/technological support from sources external to the country is terminated or considerably reduced. The associated requisites for the attainment of sustainable results include (a) the deployment of the recipient country's indigenous resources; (b) the creation of a realistic framework for the project at both the micro and macro levels; (c) the guaranteeing of political will and commitment to the project; and (d) the facilitation of the needed physical and technological resources during the life span of the project.

Aid effectiveness has been the subject of a good number of in-depth analyses during the last ten years. The most noteworthy feature from all these studies is that it is difficult to arrive at any firm conclusions as to the effecti-

[1] Studies of aid usually refer to the countries receiving aid as "recipients". This is a term which is quite illustrative of the status of the developing countries in the aid relationship.

veness of aid. In the available literature different authors come to different conclusions regarding this issue. Cassen's work "Does Aid Work" (1986) and Mosley's "Aid and Power" (1990) arrive at two different conclusions. The first suggests that aid has, in general, had a positive impact on economic development, while the latter is considerably more critical to the effects of aid. One of the oldest critics of development aid, Peter Bauer, has pointed out that there are few examples in economic history where external resource flows have been instrumental, or even necessary, for the economic development of a country.[2] In other words, if the necessary conditions for growth are absent, aid will not be very effective. Lipton and Toye's study "Does Aid Work in India?" (1991) underscores this connection between internal conditions and the effectiveness of external resources. They arrive at the conclusion that aid to India has had a positive impact, not only because aid has done the right things, but because aid has been integrated in a coherent way into the development policy of the country. A key factor in this process has been the high aid management capacity of India. Riddell takes a slightly different position in his book "Foreign Aid Reconsidered" (1987) where he points to a general problem of data. The knowledge we have about the impact of aid is not good enough for allowing us to take a firm position in one direction or the other. There is a danger of drawing general conclusions too quickly on the basis of insufficient data.

Existing studies on aid effectiveness have chosen as their focus of study, either the macro level or the micro level. Macro oriented studies represent attempts to measure whether aid has had any effects on the recipient country in terms of level of national income and the growth and distribution of that income. This has been done either by trying to aggregate results from the micro (project) level (Cassen, 1989) or by attempting to develop macro economic models for measuring the impact of aid (Mosley 1991, White and Luttik, 1994).[3] Within the aid agencies the evaluation function has usually been directed towards measuring project successes or failures, often with no ambition to provide any aggregate analysis. Their primary role has been to serve project management purposes within the agencies. Methodologically, both approaches have faced serious difficulties when attempting to measure the effectiveness of aid. One particularly interesting aspect of this problematique is the macro–micro paradox—while micro level evaluations have been able to establish mostly positive results, it is difficult to see these positive results reflected at the macro level.[4]

Mosley (1987) and White (1994) offer explanations for this paradox which has either to do with measurement techniques and data used, or fungibility of aid within the public sector, crowding out effects etc. It is, however, also

[2] Bauer, P.T., 1992, p. 100.

[3] White, H. & J. Luttik, 1994.

[4] Mosley, P., 1987, pp. 139–142.

possible to find explanations for this paradox using a strand of economic theory, where the point of departure is the institutions of a society.[5]

Institutions are important for the macro–micro paradox because they form the incentive structure of a society. Institutions structure human interaction by providing either formal and/or informal constraints. The former are the rules, law and constitutions formulated by society over time. The latter are largely unwritten rules such as norms of behaviour, conventions, self imposed codes of conduct. The political and economic institutions are the underlying determinants of economic performance. Institutions and the technology employed determine the transaction and transformation costs that add up to the costs of production.[6] An efficient market appears when transactions are without cost. When transactions are costly, then institutions become important. The requirements to approximate Coase's zero transaction cost condition are tough. Actors need to know their objectives and how to achieve them. Access to knowledge is a key requirement and this brings into focus the process whereby information from actions feeds back into new decisions.

Institutions are designed to facilitate such a process. The extent to which they manage to fulfil their task determines transaction costs, and hence economic performance.

Thus, institutions are positioned in between the micro and the macro level. They act as a filter between these two levels. If the filter is clogged with dirt and grime, little will reach the macro level in terms of impact, good or bad, from what has happened at the micro level. An efficient filter will ensure that only pure, healthy water from upstream reaches the consumers downstream and not any unwanted substances. The relationship between the three levels can be illustrated by Figure 1.1.

The figure shows how reforms at the macro level affect the micro level through a middle level—often called the meso level. It consists of more or less well-functioning markets and institutions (bureaucracies, rules, laws etc.). Through these institutions and markets signals reach the actors which provide the framework for their actions. If the signals are "correct" one can expect behaviour which is conducive to development.

At the micro level we find the individual project. At the project level we can study aid projects within sectors such as education, health, agriculture and industry. Although the importance of the traditional aid project seems to be declining, the sector based project mode has been the traditional mode of operation for aid. But during the last five years increasing attention has been paid to the macro level. By this we mean the national level where we study the impact of aid on macro economic aggregates, such as balance of payments, the gross domestic product (GDP), trade, income distribution etc.

---

[5] North, D., 1990; pp. 359–368.

[6] Coase, R., 1960, pp. 1–44.

Figure 1.1. *Linkages between the macro and micro levels*

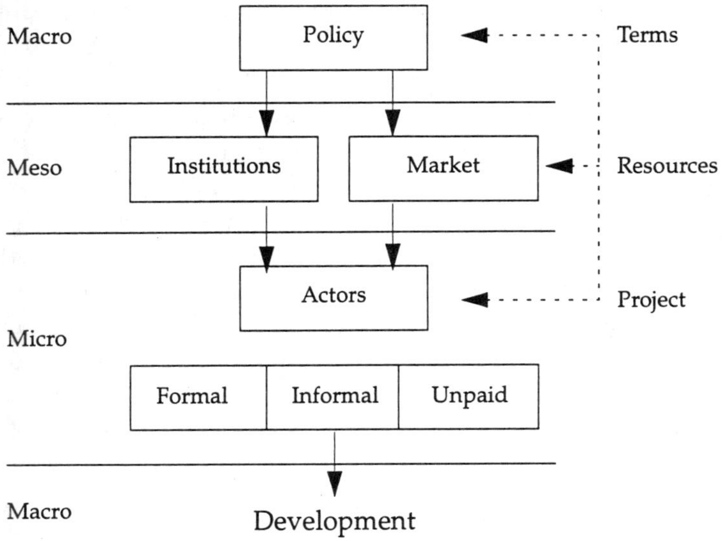

Source: Larsson, K., *Strukturanpassning. Bistånd och utveckling.* Stockholm: SIDA, 1994, p. 16.

The focus on the macro level has been motivated by the declining growth rates of most African countries. There has been a concern that in spite of successful work at the project level, there has been little evidence of positive impact at the macro level. This micro–macro paradox has focused attention on the middle level, the so called meso level. This is where we find different organisations in the host country, responsible for receiving and making productive use of aid resources. Their ability, or rather inability, to do this is now being seen as a major explanation to the micro–macro paradox. The fact that we see so little in terms of positive impact on national development from aid, can be attributed to organisations which are not operating efficiently. The effectiveness of the meso level is not merely a function of inappropriate organisations, but also a lack of proper policies and the extent to which they are applied to deal with the problems facing the country.

A review of the literature on why aid has not performed the way it was expected to soon shows that there are a number of issues which seem to surface time after time. First, the recipient has often been marginally involved in the early planning and design of a project. Donor priorities have tended to dominate and they have furthermore been erratic and inconsistent with recipient priorities. Second, recipient national institutions are inadequate to perform the tasks they are expected to perform due to political, administrative and human resource limitations. Third, aid has been poorly designed and sustainability considerations have not been sufficiently addressed by either donor or recipient. Fourth, aid conditionalities have reinforced the inequality of the aid relationship, and thereby reduced the effectiveness of aid. Fifth, the mix of forms of aid in a given recipient country tends to be donor driven and sub-optimal. Sixth, aid coordination has not been sought by either donors or recipients, and its absence has limited the effectiveness of aid. Finally, the lack of transparency and accountability among donors and recipients undermines the effectiveness of aid.

What emerges out of these issues is the primacy attached to the organisations involved in delivering and receiving aid. There is no lack of evidence, nor awareness, of the importance of institutions for aid effectiveness. Efficient organisations operating within an appropriate institutional framework are one of the key pre-conditions for sustainable and effective aid. Aid evaluations frequently point this out as a major determinant of the success or failure of aid. The organisations and structures in the host country are not strong enough to accommodate the resources that are provided through aid. The response from the aid community has also come forth. There has been a shift in their programmes towards a stronger emphasis on institution building and capacity development. Strengthening the capacity to receive is a key component in the strategy to improve aid effectiveness.

This is a conviction shared by the authors of this book. But the institutional perspective has to be widened in order to properly understand the causational factors involved. The capacity to receive is not only determined by the effectiveness of the recipients' institutions. It is also determined by the effectiveness of the donor organisations, and, as it takes two to tango, the nature of the relationship that exists between them. Thus, an institutional perspective on aid effectiveness cannot be limited to an analysis of the host country institutions and organisations only. Their effectiveness is not only determined by factors internal to them, but also by the constraints imposed on them through the interaction with other organisations and institutions.

We can now formulate the major purpose of this book. This study is not concerned with establishing how effective aid has been. Instead, we accept as prima facie evidence that aid most likely has not been as effective as expected by both donors and host countries. Our focus is instead on what we see as one of the key determinants of aid effectiveness—the aid relationship. The purpose of this book is to investigate the quality of collaboration between a donor and a host country. Our case is aid to Zambia.

In the next section we shall present the outline of the book and explain how we approached the study methodologically, before we spend time on discussing a possible theoretical framework which helps us explain the primacy of the aid relationship in determining aid effectiveness.

THE DESIGN OF THE STUDY

When approaching a subject as wide and difficult as aid effectiveness certain limitations and restrictions are in order to make the research task manageable. The first and most important concern, the choice of basic research method. One possible option was to position the study at the national level, primarily using secondary sources. This could be a way of establishing a national perspective on the situation regarding the aid relationship. For a number of reasons that method was ruled out. First, available secondary sources, which often is evaluation material, rarely discuss aid effectiveness and even more rare are discussions about the aid relationship. Second, there would be a problem of access to material. Third, given the time and resources available to us this method was not feasible. Instead we opted for a case study approach. A handful of aid interventions were used to investigate our problem. We shall not spend time outlining the methodological possibilities and restrictions of the case study approach. There is a vast literature on this subject which the reader can consult.[7] Suffice it to say that the purpose of the case studies in this study was to provide an in-depth knowledge on how the aid relationship actually worked. In the following Chapter 2, the theoretical and methodological point of departure for our study will be presented. In order to make full use of the case study approach, it is important to provide a theoretical framework which will guide us through the case studies and provide the operational tools for the analysis of the aid relationship. Such a framework is also useful for a discussion about the causal links between the aid relationship and aid effectiveness emerging out of the case studies.

Chapter 3 deals with the macro economic development of Zambia. The reader may ask if this chapter serves any other purpose than just providing a background to the case studies. Actually, it does. First of all, because a knowledge about the state of the economy helps us to explain the character and dynamics of the aid relationship. Furthermore, an analysis of the economic history of Zambia is needed to come somewhere towards understanding why there is a lack of supply response in the economy, in spite of the current donor influenced policies of structural adjustment.

This chapter also contains a short review of the possible effectiveness of balance of payments support (BOP). This is a form of programme aid which has become increasingly important over the years in Zambia. In 1993 it accounted for around half of the total aid flows to the country. Clearly, any discussion of the effectiveness of the aid relationship cannot avoid this issue. It offers a good opportunity to study the aid relationship at the macro level, and in particular the policy conditionalities involved in aid. For many reasons, one of the most important is perhaps the issue of fungibility, BOP remains one of the most difficult research areas in terms of establishing impact and effectiveness of aid. It offers, however, a lot of solid material regarding the quality of the dialogue between donors and Zambia over the years.

---

[7] Yin, R.K., 1991; Normann, R.A., 1970; Glaser, B. & A.L. Strauss, 1967; Gummesson, E.M., 1988; and Garaway, G., 1966.

Closely related to policy and macro economic issues is the question how much aid does Zambia really receive? How important is aid for the economy as a whole? Chapter 4 follows as a logical next step as it is concerned with a presentation of the magnitude of aid flows to and their utilisation by Zambia.

Chapters 5–8 forms the empirical backbone of this study and consist of four case studies of aid projects. When selecting case studies two criteria were used. First, the cases should represent a good sample of the various donors active in Zambia, multilateral as well as bilateral. Second, the cases should be projects which somehow had a "poverty orientation". The target group should be found among the poor people of Zambia. A third criterion used in the selection of projects was to allow for representation among those that have been ongoing for a long time, and are in the process of phasing out, and those that are ongoing and still working on improving their *modus operandi*.

We identified four projects which were subjected to an in-depth study. The first was a case of food aid. The 1992 emergency drought relief operation to southern Africa (DESA) represented the multilateral category. The second was a project which concerned the production and distribution of free primary and secondary school books. The Zambia Educational Materials Project (ZEMP), was and is managed by FINNIDA. This case also possessed some multilateral elements to it in the sense that another donor, SIDA, has been actively involved in the activities through the provision of financial resources. The last two cases are particularly poverty oriented in that they had the purpose of improving water supply and sanitation facilities in villages in Zambia. One case concerned the NORAD-supported Water Supply and Sanitation Programme in Western Province of Zambia. The other was the JICA-aided Groundwater Development Project in the Southern Province.

The issue of aid coordination also features prominently in this study and Chapter 9 is devoted to this aspect. The study postulates that, as an integral part of the organisational milieu of aid management, coordination within and between the donor and recipient agencies is fundamental for the effectiveness of aid. Apart from facilitating the awareness of the nature and magnitude of external support, coordination between the major actors in the aid relationship also permits meaningful utilisation of scarce resources. Similarly, coordination between the donors and recipients allows the former to receive and interpret correctly the latter's policies and priorities and, thus, reduce the generally disliked donor-driven approach to development.

The last chapter of this study, Chapter 10, analyses aid effectiveness and sustainability in the context of the experiences of the four case studies and Zambia's experiences with aid support and the institutional framework within which it is received, managed and utilised. What kind of general conclusions could be derived for the purpose of establishing an effective aid relationship and hence lay the foundations for a high aid effectiveness? Our point of departure for answering this question is to perceive the donor–recipient interaction in the context of the degree to which their organisational and institutional structures facilitate or retard the enhancement of aid effectiveness.

Chapter 2

The Effectiveness of the Aid Relationship —A Theoretical Departure

Why is the aid relationship so important in understanding the effectiveness of aid? To answer this question we need to first of all define what we actually mean by the aid relationship? Secondly, we need to situate it within a theoretical context which will help us in outlining the causational links between aid effectiveness and the aid relationship.

What then is the aid relationship? The starting point is that aid is very much a joint undertaking between a donor and a recipient country government. Aid as a unilateral activity is, at least in theory, not accepted by most donors and all recipient countries. The parties join forces in order to do something together. The aid relationship is in essence a practical thing—a working relationship. As such it can be understood as an interaction between two organisations in order to do something which is jointly agreed upon.

At a superficial level one could say that the aid relationship is important for aid effectiveness, because if the working relationship does not work, then not much will be accomplished. This is true, but unfortunately not very helpful, since it does not really clarify why this connection exists. Other than the trivial conclusion that if you want to do something with somebody else it is good if you, first, have agreed that you want to work together, second, have agreed on what you want to do together, there does not exist a unified theory which we can apply to this problem. The situation is rather that we have to use a multidisciplinary approach, enlisting the help from disciplines such as economic history, business economics and psychology.

Our starting point is the organisation (for the sake of simplicity let us assume that the aid relationship involves only two organisations). What do we mean by organisations? First of all there is a clear distinction to be made between institutions and organisations. The aid debate in particular is notorious for mixing up the two. Institution building is often used to describe an aid intervention which aims towards strengthening an organisation. Sometimes one can see a distinction based on Selzninck's idea of the institutionalised organisation. When an organisation is change-inducing, change-protecting and formal it is considered to be an institution. The organisation represents values that are considered as important by society.[8] The distinction used by us follows the definition of institutions as provided by the New Institutional Economists: a set of formal and informal constraints regulating human interaction.

Organisations can be political bodies (parties, a city council, regulatory bodies), economic bodies (firms, trade unions, family farms, cooperatives), social bodies (churches, clubs, athletic associations), educational bodies (schools, universities). Organisations are not static, they are constantly moving and changing. The issue is: what explains organisational action?

The organisations that exist reflect the opportunities and incentives provided by the institutional framework. How organisations work and people make their decisions are conditioned by the formal and informal constraints provided by the institutions. In other words, if the institutions establish the rules of the game, then the organisations are the players. But we need to take one step further into organisational life to deepen our understanding of what makes an organisation tick.

An organisation is often seen as an instrument for carrying out certain activities to reach an objective. The structure of the organisation is seen as a key factor determining the effectiveness of the organisation. Changing the structure is the way to change the efficiency of the organisation in producing its goods or services. Action is guided by reason. This is a static view of the organisation which fits badly with the real world. Our understanding of an organisation is different.

> We understand the organisation as a social construct that thinks, learns and acts through its members. An organisation lives in motion and cannot be fully understood as a static phenomenon. It is made up of relations between its actors at different levels, both within and outside the organisation. The dynamics of an organisation is made up of how people cooperate, compete or end up in conflict with each other. Thus, when constructing our picture of an organisation we may start by understanding the driving forces behind the dynamics of individual behaviour and action in organisational life. In an organisation, as in society, people think differently and act differently, and this gives rise to organisational politics.[9]

A model of the organisation as a political system—incorporating interests, conflict and power—provides a practical and systematic means of understanding the relationship between politics and organisation and emphasises the key role of power in determining political outcomes.

What happens when two organisations meet in order to do business together? Can they be expected to cooperate? When do individuals want to cooperate? What determines a good outcome from the cooperation? These are questions which lead us directly to the heart of the matter—the aid relationship.

---

8 Selznick, P., 1957; Blase, M., 1973; Moore, M., 1995/1.

9 Carlsson, J., G. Köhlin, & A. Ekbom, 1994.

The dynamics of the aid relationship can be analysed by using the political metaphor in much the same way as we would have done when analysing a single organisation. But inter-organisational cooperation adds other dimensions which influence the outcome of the cooperation. In the official rhetoric aid is often described as friendly cooperation, where two parties work for a common goal—namely the development of one of the parties. This is of course a picture which few aid practitioners find very convincing. Aid is much more complicated than that. It is a relationship which is characterised by a biased distribution of resources and heavily influenced by various stakeholder interests.

The aid relationship is a matter of power, organisational system and values, beliefs and attitudes. Power gives strength and a position for advancing ideas, interests and actions. Organisation is the way the work is set up in order to achieve the objectives of aid. But what guarantees the maximum satisfaction of the objectives? Actors have to assess possible action alternatives and then choose the one which they believe represent the best course of action. Does this mean a rational choice along the lines underlying economic theory?

Simon has pointed out that decisions are normally taken on the basis of bounded rationality. It cannot be assumed that individuals know what is in their interest and act accordingly. Especially not under conditions of uncertainty (under which aid works to a high degree). Decisions are rarely taken under conditions of perfect knowledge of all possible alternatives. Thus, there is a distinction to be made between the real world and the actors' perceptions of it and reasoning about it.[10] This suggests that what we know and what we learn is a social construct. Our knowledge structures and belief systems differ and our interpretations and explanations of what we see around us will consequently be different. It is within such belief systems learning takes place. Learning then is an incremental process filtered by the culture of a society which determines the perceived costs and benefits. At the same time knowledge and the quality of our learning are fundamental long-run sources of change. How can this apparent contradiction be reconciled? The question is particularly relevant in the context of the aid relationship where different belief systems come in direct contact with each other and obviously therefore different incentive structures determining what should be learned and why.

Our knowledge about aid effectiveness is far from perfect. We cannot say with reasonable accuracy how effective aid has been in a country. We can make well-informed guesstimates as to what are the major determinants of aid effectiveness. Aid agencies have for many years now been busy trying to develop sophisticated appraisal and evaluation systems, better methods and techniques for measurement, better trained programme officers etc., all in

---

[10] Simon, H., 1986, pp. 210–211.

order to gain more knowledge about what they are doing. Still, however, there is a large grey area of knowledge which we cannot access through any of these traditional means. The following quotation gives an idea as to where the answer to these questions can be sought:

> ... it is hardly possible to gain comprehensive knowledge of the impact of aid. Furthermore, even if we had such knowledge, it is hardly likely that it would be fed back into our learning to such an extent that aid agencies would dramatically improve their performance. The real world is not like that. No sophisticated planning schemes or economic analysis tools are able to help us achieve such a perfect world. We think, however, that it is possible to improve the present situation by changing the way we seek knowledge and exchange information. The project is an arena where different stake-holders act. The evaluation function should take note of this and allow the stake-holders a say in assessments of project performance. The evaluation function needs to be more democratic ...[11]

We understand aid as a socially constructed and negotiated process. Aid evaluation has for long been based on a concept of knowledge which implies "discovering facts", as if they were out there waiting to be uncovered. This is an approach which is based on "objectives", which assumes that the world is composed of facts and that the goal of knowledge is to provide a literal account of what the world is like.[12]

The aid relationship is an arena for communication of such constructions. It is an arena where the parties in the aid relationship exchange their models for explaining and interpreting the environment, i.e. exchanging views on what is effective aid.

It is how well this arena works with respect to such processes which is a key determinant of aid effectiveness. The functioning of the aid relationship in terms of communication and learning can not be understood only in terms of formal systems for appraisal, monitoring and evaluation. Production and transformation of knowledge are situated in the processes by which social actors interact, negotiate and accommodate to each others perceptions of the world. These processes and outcomes are shaped by sources of power, authority and legitimation available to the different actors involved.[13] As suggested above it is a highly unequal relationship which makes it susceptible to political games and conflicts. This means that conflict management becomes an important property of the aid relationship. Conflict management presupposes two things. First, that we have a toolbox which we can use for identifying different patterns of conflict. Second, that we manage to explain the causes of conflict.

In the next section we shall discuss both of these issues more carefully.

---

11 Carlsson, J., et al., ibid., p. 204.

12 Knorr-Cetina, K.D., 1981.

13 Arce, A. & N. Long, 1992, p. 214.

A CONFLICT PERSPECTIVE ON THE AID RELATIONSHIP

Traditionally, organisation theory looks at organisations as functionally well integrated and rational systems. In an administrative sense, this might be the case but organisational life cannot be understood simply in terms of bureaucratic rationality. Organisations are not like machines and organisms which are unified systems that bind part and whole together for a common goal. Rather, they are made up of individuals who work there. Indeed, the political perspective dismantles the idea of organisations as functionally integrated systems. In this respect, an organisation is perceived more as a political system built up by networks of people with divergent interests. This implies that conflict of interest becomes a more or less permanent feature of an organisation. Conflict is often regarded as something abnormal and undesirable. In real life, however, conflict is inevitable and springs from organisational changes: moving people, changing the mandate of departments, etc. Conflict will, therefore, always be there and, for that matter, should always be there; it is the prime mover behind change and development.

What is meant by conflict? In principle, conflict is incompatible behaviour between parties whose interests differ. Incompatible behaviour refers to actions by one party intended to oppose or frustrate the other party. Interests refer to recognised and unrecognised stakes that are affected by the interaction of parties.[14] Why are inter-organisational conflicts important? The answer is simple: if you don not manage the conflicts, the conflicts will manage you. Conflict at organisational interfaces often involves a mix of conflicting and common interests among the parties, and the kind of interaction may depend on the balance of interests, as perceived by the parties. Power becomes in this context a crucial variable. For the purpose of this report, power is the ability of one party to get another to behave in ways incompatible with the latter's interest. Power is exercised within organisations as well as between organisations and it is the medium through which conflicts of interest are alleviated and resolved. Some organisations are more powerful than others either because of their position in the hierarchy (formal power), or because they possess a valuable resource (informal power); money, information, etc. There are many power holders in an organisation, and some possess more power than others.

Generally speaking, there is evidence that the likelihood for inter-organisational conflict is increasing rapidly. First, organisations tend to become larger and more internally complex over time. The more numerous and diverse the levels and specialised divisions within an organisation, the more opportunities for conflict at their interfaces. Second, there is a tendency to-

14 There are two types of conflict. *Latent conflict* occurs when conflicting interests are accompanied by compatible behaviour. *False conflict* involves common interests, but incompatible behaviour.

wards increasing interdependence within and between organisations. Organisational performance is affected by the coordination of diverse departments and linkages among diverse organisations are important to their performance. The more interdependence between parties, the higher the cost of poorly managed conflict at their interface. Third, the rate of social and technological change affecting organisations and societies is still accelerating and this brings in more conflict.

CONFLICTS IN THE INTERFACE

Aid involves a number of various actors at different levels and with varying functions to perform. These actors interact through a multitude of relationships. Analysis of the aid relationship may, therefore, easily become both complex and cumbersome. The concept of *interface* offers a possibility to structure such an analysis. Interface conveys an idea of some kind of face-to-face encounter between individuals with differing interests, resources and power. Studies of interface encounters aim to bring out the types of discontinuities that exist and the dynamic and emergent character of the struggles and interactions that take place, showing how actors' goals, perceptions, values, interests and relationships are reinforced or reshaped by this process.

Interfaces contain within them many levels and forms of social linkage and discontinuity. Studies of interface should not therefore be restricted to observing what goes on during face-to-face encounters, since these interactions are in part affected by actors, institutional and cultural frameworks, and material and/or immaterial resources. In other words, as Long points out, the methodology of interface studies should focus not only on specific social interaction processes, but also be sure to situate these within broader institutional and power fields.[15]

The interface analysis takes an actor-oriented approach, which concentrates upon the interplay of different social constructions of reality developed by the various parties to the interface (government bureaucrats, aid officials, evaluators, peasant farmers, women etc.) and traces out their social implications.

Brown applies a conflict perspective on the interface analysis defines an interface as an arena where two or more organisations meet in order to collaborate. Inherent in interface dynamics is conflict. The key quality of an interface is its ability to handle conflicts in a productive way in order to maximise effectiveness. If the interface contains potential "conflict sources" or any other disturbances which it is not able/willing to manage, then effectiveness will be low.[16]

---

[15] Long, N., 1989.

[16] Brown, D.L., 1983.

Brown's general approach gives rise to three key questions which a conflict focused interface analysis should deal with. Firstly, what are the potential sources of conflict? Secondly, does the organisational interface contain mechanisms for eliminating them? If the answer to the second question is negative, then it becomes relevant to ask the third question: how should an organisational interface be designed in order to eliminate dysfunctional influences?

The aid relationship can be understood as an interface. It is an arena where organisations meet in order to conduct business. The continued interactions between organisations that are collaborating produce interfaces that are social units themselves. This is the analytical point of departure—the idea of the interface as a social unit in itself. Continued contact encourages the development of boundaries and shared expectations that regulate the interaction of interface participants. The interface itself becomes an organised entity. This is how one can understand the aid relationship—an interface with its own dynamics produced by the interaction between the aid agency and the recipient country organisations.

A closer analysis of the concept of interface would facilitate a more organised discussion of Zambia's relationship with its donors. In order to facilitate a full understanding of our analytical framework it is necessary to discuss in some detail the concept of conflict. Against the above background, it can be argued that the aid relationship is particularly conflict prone since it involves a relationship between unequal partners. One party possesses a lot of resources while the other has very few and, to a large extent, actually depends on the stronger for its operations. The issues of power and dependency, therefore, feature strongly in the aid relationship.

Organisational interfaces bring together organisations whose goals and assumptions may be very diverse, although they may depend on each other for critical information or resources. The configuration of a basic interface is shown in Figure 2.1.

Figure 2.1. *The basic interface*

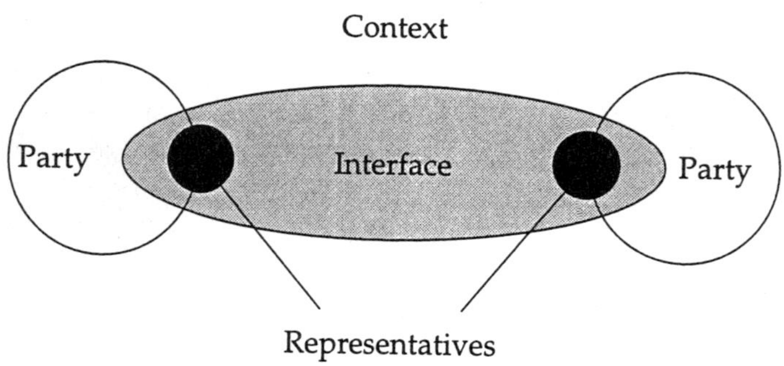

Figure 2.2. *Relationships in a typical aid project in Zambia*

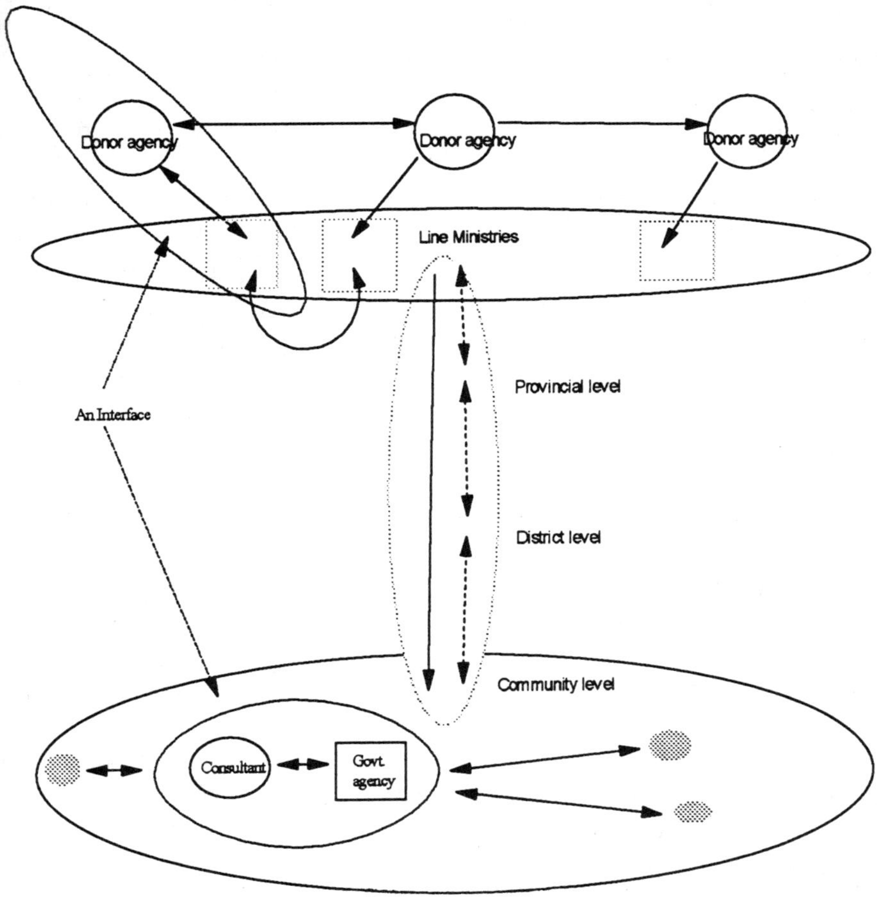

Aid is a relationship between two governments, but it should not be understood as one relationship. Instead various interfaces are constructed where the representatives of the governments meet. The aid agency is representing the donor government, while the recipient government can be represented by any government agency appropriate for the particular activity at hand, for example the Ministry of Finance. The aid relationship can therefore be described as a typical organisation interface. The aid agency in turn is represented in the interface by the local development cooperation office, or a single programme officer. The host country representative in the actual discussions in the interface can be represented by a coordinating unit; a parastatal agency; or a line ministry. But the aid relationship can also exist at other levels in the recipient country. Figure 2.2 illustrates how the aid relationship can be replicated at different organisational levels in the host country.

This is a rather fragmented arena consisting of several relationships. Although the predominant mode of interaction is found at the central level, donor agencies and their representatives can also develop interfaces with organisations at the provincial or district levels. At the community level the donor is often represented by technical experts/consultants working in a particular project, while the host government is represented through its district authorities.

Each relationship, or interface, develops its own pattern of conflict and each has to find its own solution to the conflicts. Conflict management of the overall interface, including all the sub-interfaces, is largely a matter of coordination. The "super-interface" of donor–recipient relations contains a whole spectrum of relationships which are largely uncoordinated. The central level does have the power but not always the resources/ability to perform a coordinating function. The donor's, in spite of lip-service, to the contrary, have a limited interest in coordinating among themselves, apart from a very basic type of coordination of keeping themselves informed about what the others are doing. The perceived mix of common and conflicting interests is crucial to explaining party behaviour. The possible mix is equally important for altering that behaviour. Analysis of parties' interests includes how important interdependencies are to them.

Analysis of an interface involves four elements, namely, 1) the parties to the interface; 2) the party representatives; 3) the mode of regulation of the interface; and 4) the larger context.[17]

The first element in the interface analysis is *the party*. Parties can be groups and organisations rather than individuals. In the case of aid, it is the aid agency and its counterpart organisations in the recipient country. They interact because they have a common task to carry out—prepare, plan and implement aid activities.

The relevant internal characteristics of parties may take on two extremes. At one end, there are groups and organisations which display clearly relevant internal characteristics: high internal cohesion; concern with tasks; relatively autocratic leadership; tight structure; and member conformity and loyalty to present a "united" front.[18] At the other end, there are parties with low cohesion; high concern for people; relatively democratic leadership; loose structure; and a "fragmented front". These parties may be more prone to avoiding differences and conflict at interfaces. Who then are *the parties in the aid relationship*?

In the aid relationship, the parties are, on the one hand, the donor agency and, on the other hand, the responsible government organisation(s) (the donor may have to deal with several parties, which in itself introduces a de-

---

[17] This framework is similar to other efforts to analyse conflict. See Adams, S., 1976; Thomas, J.M. & W.G. Bennis, 1972; and Katz, D. & R.L. Kahn, 1978.

[18] Schein, E., 1970.

gree of complexity). The donor agency and the host organisation are fairly similar. On the continuum from being overorganised to underorganised, both tend to lean towards the former. They are both centralised organisations with procedures and rules that regulate their activities. This does not, however, exclude a considerable level of decentralisation of decision-making that gives programme officers quite some influence on the course of action of the agency. This introduces a certain degree of looseness in the organisation, which is both a strength and a weakness. A strength in the sense that it facilitates the prompt handling of new problems and unforeseen situations. It is a weakness to the extent that it may introduce some confusion as to who actually represents the organisation.

The second element in the interface is *the representatives of the parties*. The parties interact with each other through their representatives. A typical example of such units in the aid system is the local office of the aid agency. An agency like FINNIDA or SIDA is normally represented by its local development office, or programme officers at headquarters. The exact demarcation of their responsibilities are quite clear in theory, but this may not always be the case in practice. Actual negotiations at organisational interfaces are carried out by individuals who represent the parties.

Events at the interface are influenced by the roles individuals occupy and their personal skills and characteristics. Duties may overlap and, consequently, confusion enter into the interface. At the recipient side, one finds special aid coordination units, national planning commissions, etc. But rarely is the host government represented by lower level personnel in the administrative hierarchy. At this level, there are also the overlapping of duties, unclear division of responsibilities, etc. The skills of individual representatives also influence events at the interface. Different bargaining and problem-solving tactics can be employed by the actors.

The third characteristic concerns the *mode of regulation of an interface.* Interface organisation reflects its capacity to constrain or guide events within it. There is a continuum of possibilities, from overorganised to being underorganised. The type of regulation prevailing at the interface depends very much on the type of regulation found in the organisations that constitute the interface.[19]

Turning now to the structural characteristics of the two principal modes of regulation, one notes, firstly, that the internal regulation of *underorganised interfaces* is excessively loose. There is little agreement about who has autho-

[19] Organisations create procedures, roles and even departments to control inputs and outputs of critical information, personnel and materials. They must also provide some internal regulation over the interaction of their subunits, if subunits are to continue to perform tasks and solve problems efficiently. For organisations that face well-understood problems, stable environments, or situations demanding rapid and well-coordinated responses, relatively tight regulation may be desirable. Organisations that face novel problems, or have low influence over their participants, may require relatively loose regulation of activity.

rity, and interface goals are undefined or conflicting. Formal regulatory mechanisms are not well-developed while representative roles are fragmented, conflictual, or undefined. The combination of open external boundaries and loose internal regulation provides little direction or guidance for representatives. Several problems are characteristic within underorganised interfaces. Resources are typically in short supply and the interface lacks personnel, information, energy and time. Available energy is diffused by the lack of a clear focus. Differences easily lead to two forms of conflict permitted by loose organisation, namely, withdrawal from differences; and escalation of conflict.

In *overorganised* interfaces, there are well-defined rules and regulations. External boundaries are comparatively closed and regulation of internal activity is tight. This limits the discretion and flexibility of the representatives. Information is not easily imported or exported while interface mechanisms hamper entry and exit of representatives. Sufficiently impermeable boundaries may slow interface response to a crawl. The internal regulation of overorganised interfaces is correspondingly tight. Leadership is centralised and unquestioned while interface goals are well-defined, unambiguous and conservative. Formal mechanisms clearly constrain activity. Roles are well-defined and enforced and rules are detailed, well-understood and seldom violated. Informal expectations also guide behaviour. Theories and values are shared among all representatives. Beliefs in the continuation of the interface and the dependability of leadership prevail. The combination of closed boundaries and tight regulation severely restricts the representatives' discretion at overorganised interfaces and activity is largely predictable. Several problems are characteristic of overorganised interfaces. Innovations are in short supply, which presents serious problems when contexts and parties face rapid change. Representatives' energies are well-directed within traditional paths, but suppressed if they move in other directions. Overt conflict tends to be suppressed by tight organisation and closed boundaries, often resulting in little productive examination of differences.

In terms of mode of organisation, it is hard to generalise about the aid relationship. Most probably it comes closer to the overorganised interface than the underorganised. Aid agencies in general are highly structured in terms of rules and procedures. But there are exceptions. Host country administrations are equally bureaucratic. This introduces certain constraints in terms of openness and flexibility.

The fourth element is *the context of the interface*. The context is the whole field within which both interface and parties are embedded. One can distinguish between the immediate and the larger context. The immediate context includes the larger social units of which the parties are sub-units. The immediate context may be complex, simple, stable or changing. Organisational interaction is sometimes closely circumscribed by the immediate context. The larger context, on the other hand, includes social, legal, economic and political forces that create opportunities for, and constraints on, the interface. Third parties are social units interested, but not directly involved, in interface events. The effects of the larger context may be difficult to predict or even recognise in events at the interface. Trends in the larger context often baffle the most sophisticated analysts, and few social units have the resources to track all the trends that might influence their futures. Studies of social conflict suggest that understanding large-scale contextual forces may be critical to understanding the problems involved at the interface. Trends in the larger context seem to be toward increased uncertainty, increased interdependence, and increased complexity and vulnerability in a civilisation based on world-wide linkages among organisations.

The context of the aid interface contributes to a significant degree to its complexity. Primarily because there is more than one context. Surrounding the donor–host country interface is an immediate context and the larger context. From the perspective of the individual donor, the immediate context is, first and foremost, other donors active in the country. The donor–host country interface is not independent of what they do. New programmes, policies, etc., do have an impact on the bilateral discussions between one donor and the host country.

The larger context can, paradoxically, be said to have an even larger impact on the aid interface. This is the country context and it includes a lot of parties with an immediate interest and influence on a particular donor– host country relationship. In many cases, these factors have been quite important in shaping the dialogue of the interface. To the larger context can be added the country context of the donor. Aid policies, budgetary crises, etc., have had an impact on shaping a donor's policy vis-à-vis the host country.

INTERFACE ACTION

In the preceding section we presented the concept of interface, its components and tried to give an idea as to how the typical aid interface would look. We shall now turn to the dynamics that takes place in the interface. An interface is not something static, it is packed with action. What kind of action takes place in the interface and what are the consequences?

Interaction between parties can lead to many forms of interface action: *problem-solving, bargaining, escalation, withdrawal* and *suppression*. These actions are associated with different conflict patterns. Figure 2.3 shows various patterns of interface action associated with conflict dynamics among organisational representatives.

This is a set of possible actions, it is used for describing what goes on in the interface. It is important to point out that this typology cannot be used for explaining why a certain conflict pattern emerges in an interface. We did previously suggest that the aid relationship is highly prone to conflicts and we gave the reasons for that. Following our presentation of the findings from the case studies we shall come back to the important issue: why do certain conflict patterns occur and not others? But before that, let us proceed with outlining each option in the typology and its consequences.

Figure 2.3. *Conflict patterns at organisational interfaces*

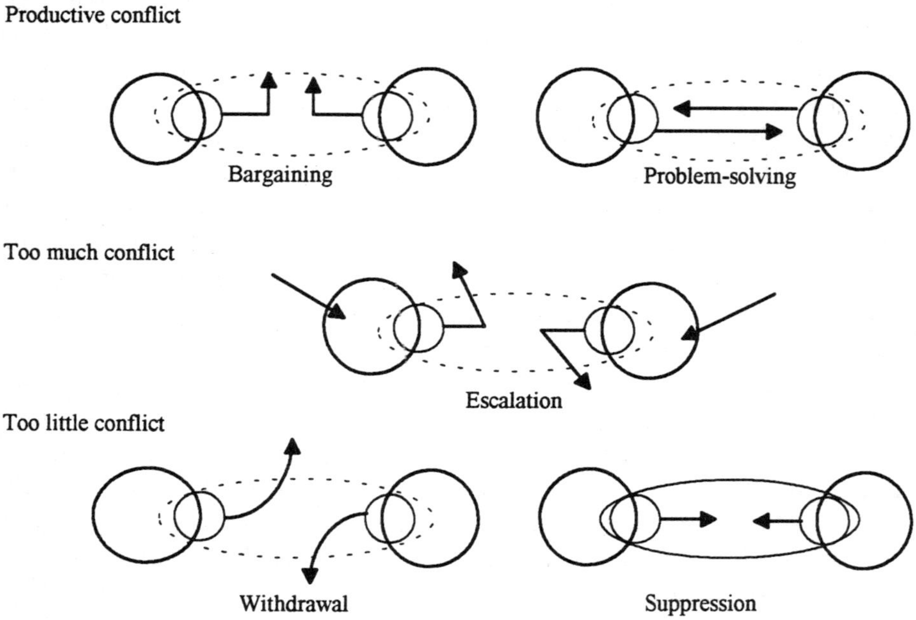

Source: Brown, L.D., *Managing Conflict at Organizational Interfaces*. Reading, Massachusetts: Addison-Wesley Publishing Company, 1983, p. 44.

PRODUCTIVE CONFLICT

Productive conflict at organisation interfaces takes the principal form of either inter-organisational bargaining or problem-solving. Representatives may engage in bargaining when they respond primarily to conflicting interests, and in problem-solving if they respond primarily to common interest. In most situations, representatives have considerable latitude for seeing the conflict in either bargaining or problem-solving terms. Either pattern may be relatively stable, maintaining similar levels of conflict over long periods of time.

Inter-organisational bargaining involves the representatives' recognition of both conflicting and common interests but focuses on issues in which one organisation's gain is perceived to be tied to another's loss. Bargaining often involves suspicion or distrust, guarded or distorted information exchanges, and "hard-ball" tactics of influence. Bargaining relations may be antagonistic and confrontative since the issues focus on conflicting interests, but representatives accept shared limits that encourage compromise and controlled escalation (negotiating arrows).

Inter-organisational problem-solving brings together organisational representatives in circumstances dominated by issues in which common interests are perceived as more important than conflicting interests. Problem-solving, in turn, often involves trust and friendliness among representatives, open and accurate exchanges of information, and largely cooperative tactics. It is also associated with moderately organised interfaces, relatively open to information sharing (long arrows) that produces mutually beneficial outcomes. As close as you can get to a situation of no conflicts at all.

Both patterns involve moderately organised interfaces (dashed boundaries) that control inputs and outputs and limit representatives' interactions. In productive conflict patterns, both multi-cultural bargaining and multi-cultural problem-solving bring together moderately organised parties able to take in new information but also able to recognise and act on behalf of their own interests (dashed boundaries). These parties interact within a clearly defined and moderately organised interface that limits debate without suppressing differences or permitting avoidance. Problem-solving interactions (long arrows) involve open exchanges of information, trust and friendliness, and exploration of options that generate mutually beneficial outcomes and understandings. Bargaining interactions (compromising arrows) involve guarded exchanges of information, suspicion and perception of differences, and manipulation, coercion and defensive tactics for creating compromise on options where perceived interests conflict.

Problem-solving and bargaining may both produce productive conflict between representatives. But any of them can also produce negative outcomes. Bargaining may produce problems of too much conflict while problem-solving can produce problems of too little conflict. This is also linked to failures of perceiving and explicitly recognising cultural differences, fostering communication about those differences when relevant, and encouraging representatives to resolve differences without escalation, suppression, or avoidance of conflict.

TOO MUCH CONFLICT

This type of interface development is often associated with inter-organisational warfare. Conflict escalation among organisational representatives is associated with organisations that are highly mobilised to fight and with an underorganised interface (dotted boundary). There are few mechanisms available for conflict management. Representatives' actions produce escalating conflict (divergent arrows) that further mobilises the organisations and further disorganises the interface. The arrows meet head-on and bounce away in different directions.

In interaction patterns characterised by too much conflict, representatives' perceptions and actions combine to create increasing distance and escalating tensions. Cultural polarisation is a feature of a too much conflict scenario. Highly mobilised cultural parties square off within a poorly defined and underorganised interface and recruit allies from the larger context (arrows from outside) to support escalating conflict.

TOO LITTLE CONFLICT

Interfaces characterised by too little conflict may develop in two different ways. The result can be withdrawal, whereby the parties try to avoid problematic differences by deliberately limiting their interaction. Interface dynamics may also result in suppression whereby parties deny their differences and act as if their interests were all common. This pattern can be hidden behind a pattern of problem-solving. Parties walk away with a feeling of agreement (or disillusion). Too little conflict between organisational representatives can be linked to the suppression of differences that compromises the autonomy of one or both parties.

The likelihood that suppression or withdrawal will occur depends on whether the interface is tightly or loosely regulated. Over-organised interfaces (solid boundary) constrain the expression and exploration of differences (truncated arrows) and results in *suppression* to the point of eroding the autonomy of one or both organisations. Interfaces that tightly organise interaction between organisations may constrain the exploration of organisational differences to such an extent that they can no longer pursue separate interests or respond to changing conditions. The outcome is inter-organisational collusion. Suppression of conflict reduces flows of information, propagates myths and stereotypic perceptions of other parties, and constricts areas for activity and innovation.

Too little conflict can also result in *withdrawal* in the form of inter-organisational isolation. This is associated with an underorganised interface (dotted boundary) that permits organisational representatives to withdraw from differences (arrows away) into a false sense of organisational independence. Under-organised interfaces permit avoidance of tensions that, in the long run, reinforce interface underorganisation and problems of interdependence that might have been averted by more engagement. Organisations can fail to recognise interdependencies, avoid interaction that would produce disagreement and reduce engagement that would help them recognise and manage common problems. In such situations, representatives in general are unwilling to discuss difficulties. Representatives who broached problems are reassured or politely ignored. Representatives that are happy with the status quo perpetuate it largely in ignorance of others dissatisfactions.

The options of withdrawal or suppression are also linked to matters of culture. There are two possibilities. There is cultural homogenisation in which cultural differences are ignored and suppressed so that potentially valuable perspectives remain unexplored. There is also cultural isolation whereby representatives withdraw from interaction at the expense of their organisationally defined interdependence.

Let us now summarise the main features of our approach for analysing the aid relationship. Two concepts have been introduced and will be used to structure the analysis of our empirical material: organisation interface and conflict. Why have they been chosen? What are their advantages respectively disadvantages?

What is the particular strength of interface analysis? First of all, interface analysis focuses on the linkage between parties rather than on the parties themselves. Second, it highlights the evolution over time of linkages. Third, interface analysis encourages attention on forces for interface integration and disintegration. In other words, interface analysis provides a framework for a dynamic, not static, analysis of relationships between organisations. The concept of organisational interface provides a set of analytical categories whereby the aid arena can be analysed and understood.

Conflict is a more or less permanent feature of the interface. But there are different types of conflicts, each with their own impact on the development of the interface. A conflict pattern characterised by too much conflict contains a good potential for escalation of the conflict and full-scale inter-organisational warfare. The outcome is immobilisation and possible disintegration of the interface. Too little conflict, on the other hand, leads to either an impasse (where the parties withdraw from interaction) or it may result in a state of suppression where the parties deny their conflicts and act as if there were none. Thus, too much or too little conflict is equally harmful for the effectiveness of the interface.

The ideal state of an interface is to find itself in a state of productive conflict. In this regard, it is important to bear in mind that the objective is not to reduce conflict. Interfaces typically exhibit moderately open boundaries and moderate internal regulation. In productive bargaining or problem-solving, there is enough control of boundary permeability to ensure the exchange of relevant inputs and outputs without permitting disruption or leakage. There is also enough internal regulation to prevent escalation or withdrawal.

CONCLUSIONS

Let us now summarise the main features of our approach for analysing the aid relationship. We have chosen the concept of interface to study the aid relationship. The starting point is that by using the concept of interface the aid relationship becomes more than just two organisations collaborating. It becomes an organisational entity in it own right, with its own rules and regulations. The concept possesses certain strong points which make it suitable for studying the situation of inter-organisational collaboration. First of all, interface analysis focuses on the linkage between parties rather than on the parties themselves. Second, interface analysis encourages attention on forces for interface integration and disintegration. Third, it provides a framework for a dynamic, not static, analysis of relationships between organisations. Conflict is a more or less permanent feature of the interface.

Within the analytical framework of interface analysis it is possible to identify a set of factors determining the action that takes place in the interface, as well as its outcome. Figure 2.4. is a simple illustration of the whole analytical framework.

Figure 2.4. *The basic framework of the interface analysis*

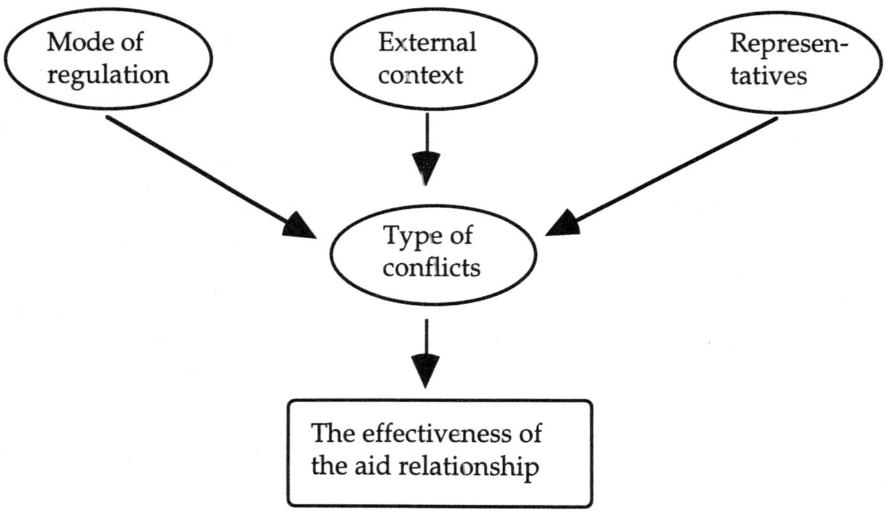

There are three key questions which a conflict focused interface analysis should deal with.

Firstly, what kind of conflict pattern is pre-dominant? There are different types of conflicts, each with their own impact on the development of the interface. A conflict pattern characterised by too much conflict contains a good potential for escalation of the conflict and full-scale inter-organisational warfare. The outcome is immobilisation and possible disintegration of the interface. Too little conflict, on the other hand, leads to either an impasse (where the parties withdraw from interaction) or it may result in a state of suppression where the parties deny their conflicts and act as if there were none. Thus, too much or too little conflict is equally harmful for the effectiveness of the interface.

Secondly, does the organisational interface contain mechanisms for management of conflicts? How should an organisational interface be designed in order to handle effectively dysfunctional influences? In this regard, it is important to bear in mind that the objective is not to reduce conflict. Rather to strive towards an interface which finds itself in a state of productive conflict.

Thirdly, effective conflict management requires an analysis that goes beyond a mere description of existing conflict patterns, modes of regulation etc. It is important to bring out the fundamental factors that cause the particular configuration of an interface.

The effectiveness of the aid relationship is thus determined by four factors: the mode of regulation of the interface; the conflict pattern; the representatives, and; the external context of the interface. They will serve an operational purpose in the sense that the purpose of our case studies will be to shed some light on each of them, thus helping us to draw some tentative conclusions as to what shapes the effectiveness of aid projects and programmes. This will then be used for providing some recommendations as to how the aid relationship can be improved.

This then concludes the presentation of our theoretical approach. We shall now turn to the reality of aid to Zambia. In the next chapter we focus on the troubled economy of the country and its structural features and development. This provides the necessary background for the subsequent analysis of the aid relationship and aid effectiveness.

Chapter 3

Macroeconomic Development in Zambia

INTRODUCTION

This chapter provides the macroeconomic background to the analysis of aid effectiveness in Zambia. The country's economic stress over the years is one of the most pronounced in Africa. The chapter traces the general economic trends from the time of political independence in 1964 to the present day. The implications of the economic adversity on the various sectors of the economy are also analysed. The policy responses of the government to the economic difficulties are presented in the last part of the chapter. The analysis begins with a general presentation of Zambia's macro economic conditions.

THE MACROECONOMIC ENVIRONMENT

Perhaps the picture of Zambia's politico-economic experience over the years since 1964 is best captured in the quotation below:

> Since Independence Zambia has gone through three distinctive economic regimes: the 1960s were relatively prosperous and with huge mineral incomes the state hoped to be able to diversify the economy. In the 1970s a number of economic shocks hit Zambia and put a stop to the ambitious agenda. The weaknesses of the economy were suddenly exposed: overdependence on mining, neglect of the rural sector and a capital-intensive, import-dependent manufacturing sector. The economic policy of the 1970s sought to maintain status quo. Economic decline, however, continued into the 1980s and it was realised that tough measures had to be embarked on in order to bring about long-term structural change. The period marked increased conflicts with regard to the economic and political agenda. Groups that hitherto had benefited from the "control regime" resisted the liberalisation efforts, while on the other hand businessmen outside these groups supported the changes. In trying to satisfy the contending views, the government failed to formulate a sustainable long-term strategy. The mix of IMF/World Bank and "own" policies has had few positive results. Today the country is groping its way through the debt burden, high inflation and the domestic demands for multi-party democracy.[20]

When Zambia attained political independence, its mineral resources were well developed. During the ten years that followed , the country's expenditure reflected its steady and considerable export receipts mainly derived

---

[20] Andersson, P & S. Kayizzi-Mugerwa, 1994.

from the copper mining sector. The country's economic performance declined significantly after 1974 following the fall in copper prices on the world market. Between 1974 and 1988, for example, Zambia's external receipts from metal products declined by 23%. Copper production in particular collapsed largely as a result of the increase in overburden to ore ratios in the open-pit mines. The growing difficulty in accessing mineral deposits worsened the situation. This state of affairs, complemented by accelerated domestic inflation, prevented the needed re-investments in the mining sector's activities to enable the country to sustain its mineral output levels. With respect to value added, the mining sector's output declined by as much as 33% over the 1974–85 period.[21] It was, thus, not surprising that mineral revenue as a proportion of GDP declined from 3.8% in 1975 to well below 2% over the 1975–85 period. Table 3.1 gives the profile of the copper sector performance over the 1965 to 1993 period and confirms the disappointing trend in all the important indicators.

Table 3.1. *The copper sector performance, 1965–1993*

	Output (tonnes)	Share of GDP (%)	Mineral tax as % of total revenue[1]	Share of exports (%)	Price per pound (US cents)[2]
1965–69	653	42.3	60.8	93	194
1970–74	683	29.4	30.0	94	154
1975–79	651	14.2	3.2	91	83
1980–84	578	14.0	3.2	92	75
1985–89	459	14.0	8.2	85	73
1990–93	418	7.5	12.0	82	80

[1] excludes grants
[2] constant 1982 prices
Source: Adam, C. et al., *Evaluation of Swedish Development Cooperation with Zambia*. Stockholm: SASDA, 1994, p.111.

Considering the country's heavy dependence on the copper mining sector and the latter's poor performance, the economy continued to slide over the 1980 to 1992 period. GDP growth in real terms during the 1980 to 1992 period is represented in Figure 3.1.

As a result of the worsening economic situation, government revenue declined sharply from 28% of GDP in 1975 to less than 18% by 1989. The situation hardly changed after that. For example, the central government's financial position declined in 1991 with a 115% increase in the overall deficit on commitment basis. The 1991 deficit was recorded at K21.7 billion, equivalent to 10% of the current GDP. This compared very unfavourably to the 1990 amount of K10.1 billion (or 8.9% of GDP).

---

[21] Saasa, O., 1994.

Figure 3.1. *Growth in real GDP, 1980–1992*

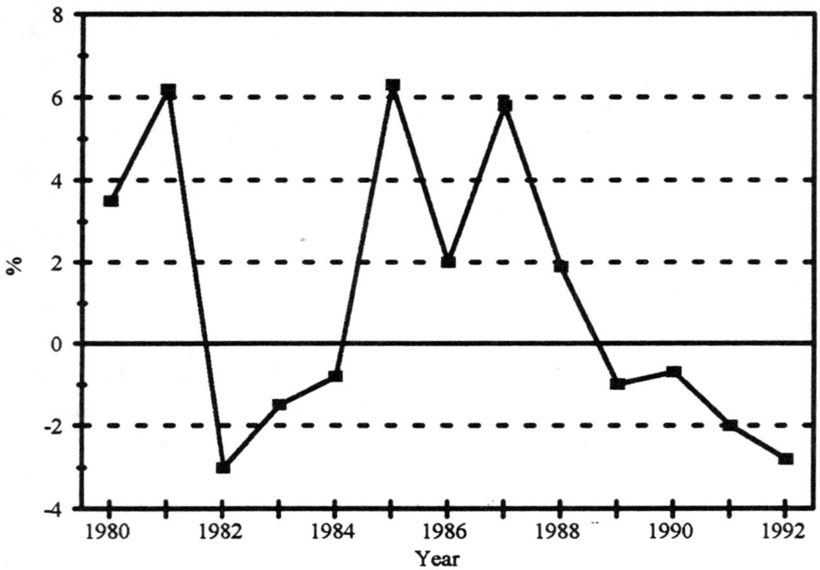

Source: Andersson, P. & M. Ndulo, *Hyperinflation, Stabilisation, and the New Economic Recovery Program*. Mimeo. Department of Economics. University of Gothenburg, 1994.

The above poor economic picture suggested the mounting difficulties that were faced by the former government in matching recurrent expenditure with internally-derived revenue and external grants. The 1991 estimates showed that external resource inflow to the government budget stood at K7.8 million while receipts from short-term loans were about K20 billion.

It is noteworthy that during its first year in office, the new government of Chiluba managed to reduce the fiscal deficit from 6.1% of the GDP in 1991 to 3.5% in 1992. This major reduction was explained largely by the substantial removal of agricultural subsidies. However, the fiscal success was adversely affected by the severe drought that affected the whole southern African region in 1992 which resulted in the need for substantial grain imports. This development, taken together with the government decision in 1992 to increase civil service salaries by 150%, largely explained the high rate of inflation in that year compared to the previous years. Table 3.2 gives the summary of the Zambian government's budget deficit, growth in money supply, and inflation rates over the 1985–93 period.

It is noteworthy that, in spite of the mining sector being the main foreign exchange earner, in terms of GDP contribution, the economy is dominated by the service sector. The most important sub-sectors are community, social and personal services; wholesale and retail trade; real estate and business services; transport, storage and communication; and restaurants and hotels. In 1991, the services sector accounted for around 44% of total GDP. It was followed by manufacturing industry with 30%, agriculture with 18% and mining with around 7.5%.[22] Thus, the "productive" sectors accounted for around 55% of total GDP. The performance of these three sectors since the mid-80s is shown in Table 3.3.

Table 3.2. *Zambian government budget deficit, growth in money supply, and inflation rates* (percentages)

	Govt. Budget Deficit/GDP	Money supply growth rates	Inflation rates
1985	-7.3	23.5	58.7
1986	-15.9	93.1	35.2
1987	-8.9	54.3	48.0
1988	-8.7	61.6	57.0
1989	-3.9	65.2	158.0
1990	-6.7	45.5	106.8
1991	-6.1	95.0	111.1
1992	-3.5	98.0	191.2
1993	-2.5	107.2	138.3
1994			35.1*

* 1994 figure quoted from the 1995 Budget Speech
Source: GRZ (Government of the Republic of Zambia), *Adjustment in Africa: The Zambian experience.* Paper Presented by the Ministry of Finance/Bank of Zambia to the World Bank Seminar on Adjustment in Africa, Harare, 1994.

Table 3.3. *Sectorial growth rates, 1986–1993*

	1986	1987	1988	1989	1990	1991	1992	1993
Agriculture	9.2	-1.7	16.5	-0.4	-7.3	4.9	-49.0	52.0
Mining	-5.0	4.4	-12.9	-9.5	2.9	1.2	12.0	-1.0
Manufacturing	0.9	8.8	18.2	1.3	-3.5	-10.7	-4.2	6.0
Total	0.7	2.7	6.3	1.0	-0.4	-1.8	-2.8	4.0

Source: Andersson, P. & M. Ndulo, *Hyperinflation, Stabilisation, and the New Economic Recovery Program*, Mimeo. Department of Economics. University of Gothenburg, 1994.

Growth rates have been sluggish, and erratic, for all sectors. The 1990s have been particularly bad for manufacturing and the agriculture sector, while mining has managed to show some positive signs.

Behind this negative growth experience lies a combination of structural weaknesses, inappropriate policies, and, at times, bad weather. The developments between 1992 and 1993 can serve as an illustration of how these various influences interact to produce a contracting economy. The GDP growth target for 1992 was 2%, but it turned out to be -2.8%. This dismal performance can be explained by a number of factors. Firstly, agriculture was hit by the earlier mentioned severe drought which resulted in a sectoral

22 UNDP, 1992.

growth rate of -49% in 1992. Good rainfall in 1993 resulted in a bumper harvest of 15 million bags of maize, thus registering a real growth of 52%. In spite of the positive agricultural yield, many farmers, particularly those in the small-scale category, were generally unable to respond promptly to the price incentive introduced by the decontrolled agricultural regime. The floor prices set by the government were perceived in many cases as some kind of "controlled" prices. The liberalisation of agricultural marketing, therefore, resulted during the transitional period in uncertainty, rather than in stimulating production.[23]

Secondly, the manufacturing sector continued to slide and recorded a growth rate of -4.2% in 1992. This was largely explained by high inflation; the squeeze in the financial markets; increasing import prices; rising interest rates; and competition from imported consumer goods. In particular, the liberalisation of the financial markets had a severe immediate impact on the productive sectors. The real value of domestic credit to the private sector, for example, fell in a significant way. In addition, the introduction of treasury bills implied a crowding out of the private sector on the financial market. Furthermore, inflation was over 190% in 1992. Altogether, the economic stress that Zambia was experiencing was devastating in its effects on the manufacturing industry sector.[24] The situation improved slightly in 1993 when the sector experienced, for the first time in three years, a positive growth rate. Growth was, however, not evenly distributed between the manufacturing sector's sub-sectors. Foodstuffs, beverages and tobacco recovered, as did chemicals, rubber and plastics, and fabricated metal products. Textiles declined by over 20% from the previous year mainly due to stiff competition from imported second-hand clothing. Wood and paper also recorded negative growth rates.

Thirdly, among the "productive" sectors, it was only mining that managed to achieve a respectable growth rate of 12%. This was not, however, enough to counteract the decline of agriculture and industry. Copper production reached 432,000 tons and the price was reasonable at an average of US$ 1.04/lb. The situation was reversed in 1993 when the prospects for the mining sector deteriorated . Copper prices dropped to 72 cents/lb and there was no sign of any recovery since stocks at the London Metal Exchange reached a 15-year high. It was estimated that the copper price would stay around 90 cents/lb during the following 5 years.[25] The low copper price; the

[23] The old system of administratively controlled prices was cancelled in 1989, except initially for maize and fertiliser. Agricultural producer prices for major crops other than maize were converted into floor prices. Consequently, all producer prices were increased considerably.

[24] In a survey made by the BOZ, it was found that out of 60 manufacturing firms, only 26% exploited bank borrowing as their main source of funding working capital. The survey also found that high input costs and lack of demand were the most serious constraints to growth.

[25] Economist Intelligence Unit, 1993.

curious Kwacha appreciation in 1993; and the low production levels combined to cause a financial crisis for ZCCM in 1993.[26]

The stagnation of the economy was further evidenced by the investment and savings level. Gross domestic investment in the Zambian economy has declined since the early 1980s. Between 1981–86, the annual investment average was 17.2% of GDP. This ratio then fell to 12.8% in the period 1987 to 1991.[27] An important consideration when assessing investments involves the relationship between public and private investments. In a situation of competition for scarce credits, a reduction in public investment might be a condition for an increase in private investments. On the other hand, an increase in public investments might be needed in order to raise private investments. In Zambia, it can be argued that private investment was crowded out by public investment during the nationalisation process of the late 1960s and early 1970s. Since then, the government has played an important role in capital formation. During the 1966–70 period, the public sector contribute 68% of total capital investments. However, the size of public investments has declined considerably since the first oil crisis in 1974.

Figure 3.2. *Private and public investment as a percentage of GDP, 1980–89*

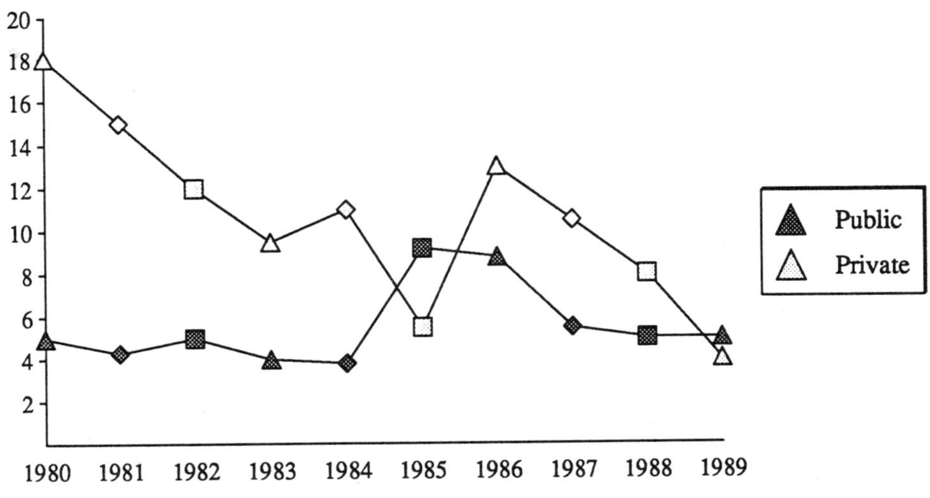

Source: Andersson, P. & M. Ndulo, *Structural Adjustment, Inflation and Political Commitment in Zambia: A Short Analysis of the New Economic Programme of 1989*. Macroeconomic Studies 28/92. Stockholm: SIDA, 1992, p.1.

26 The company was unable to meet its obligations to local suppliers and to the government. A rescue package was arranged, amounting to 7 billion Kwacha, plus other short-term facilities from local banks. One of the effects could be a further crowding out of the private sector from the financial markets.

27 World Bank, 1994, Table A.23, p. 250.

According to Figure 3.2, public investment remained low during the first four years of the 1980s. It increased during the SAP period (1985–86) to reach 9.2% of GDP. However, it declined again after the reintroduction of the control economy in 1987 to as low as 3.5% by 1989. The private sector reacted positively to the 1985 to early 1987 liberalisation stance as confirmed by the sudden increase in investments. The rise in investments in 1986 was principally due to businessmen being able to easily access foreign exchange through the auctioning system. Consequently, many investors did increase their stock holdings. However, the return to the controls regime reversed the positive pattern that was setting in.

Savings experienced a similar trend. Gross domestic savings fell from 14.1% of GDP in the period 1981–1986 to 13.4% in the period 1987–1991. Public savings were actually negative for most of the period, implying that savings mainly took place in the private sector. When these figures are matched with private consumption, which increased its share of GDP, and private savings (that has declined to a very low level), the following conclusions can be made:

- private entrepreneurs had a limited confidence in government policies;
- private economic agents were severely affected by the economic decline in the country; and
- capital flight out of the country is probably of a considerable size.

Another noteworthy phenomenon in Zambia's macroeconomic trends regards the economy's considerable external imbalances . During the 1980s and early 1990s the Zambian economy continued to experience considerable imbalances in its external account. As Figure 3.3 shows, however, there has been a steady reduction in the deficit since the mid-80s. In 1985–86 the current account deficit amounted to 17% of the GDP.

During the 1990s, the situation has improved considerably. The deficit has varied between 2–3% of the GDP. Zambia's basic problem with her external accounts can be illustrated with the situation in 1992.

The balance of trade in that year was positive but it reflected a very weak trade structure. Copper earnings accounted for 78% of total export proceeds. When cobalt and zinc are included, minerals accounted for about 90% of the country's export receipts. The surplus in the trade account was, however, wiped out by the deficit in the services account. This deficit had been primarily caused by non-factor service payments and a net investment outflow. This was partly balanced by the receipt of unrequited transfers from abroad, which left the current account balance at a deficit of US$ 79.4 million. Table 3.4 gives the balance of payments picture for 1992. The 1992 performance clearly compared unfavourably with the previous year. For example, whereas the country's trade surplus in 1991 was estimated at US$ 357.3 million, it declined by 60% in 1992.

Figure 3.3. *Current account as a percentage of GDP, 1980–1992*

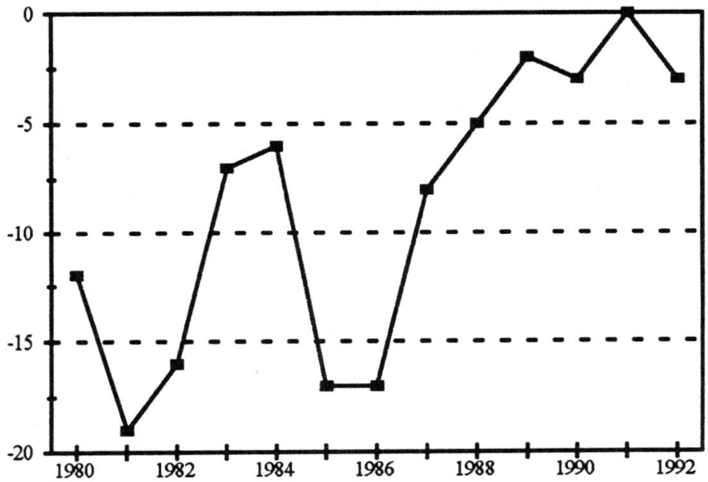

Source: GRZ (Government of the Republic of Zambia), *Monthly Digest of Statistics*, various issues; GRZ, *Budget Address*, various years; GRZ, *Economic Review*, Lusaka: NCDP, 1992; and IMF, *Government Finance Statistics*, various years.

Table 3.4. *Balance of payments in 1992*

Item		US$ Million	
1. Exports (fob)			1,203.6
of which:	Copper	940.4	
	Cobalt	132.7	
	Zinc	7.7	
	Other traditional	5.9	
	Non-traditional	116.9	
2. Imports (fob)			829.3
of which:	Crude oil	128.7	
	Fertiliser	23.4	
	Other imports	677.2	
3. Trade balance			374.3
4. Non-factor services (net)			-250.0
of which:	Freight & insurance	-122.1	
	Other services	-127.9	
5. Investment income (net)			-510.8
6. Unrequited transfers			307.1
7. Service account			-453.7
8. Current account balance			-79.4

Source: GRZ (Government of the Republic of Zambia), *Economic Review*. January–June 1993. Lusaka: NCDP, 1993.

Most Sub-Saharan African economies faced deteriorating terms of trade between 1970 and 1986. Non-oil exporters suffered losses of about 30% while mineral exporters were even harder hit, with losses of about 50%. According to a recent study of the World Bank, although the worsening terms of trade hindered growth, they were not decisive in Africa's stagnation and decline. Even for Zambia, probably the region's hardest-hit country, terms-of-trade deterioration explains only 1% of the 3.4% reduction in annual GDP growth.[28]

The deficit in the services account is closely linked to Zambia's debt burden. Table 3.5 gives the development of Zambia's external debt.

Table 3.5. *Zambia's external debt situation*

Year	Total debt	as % of GDP	as % of exports
1970	627	36	63
1975	1,137	49	129
1980	2,182	61	134
1985	4,637	178	554
1986	5,707	317	769
1987	6,599	315	695
1988	6,832	200	550
1989	6,739	235	826
1990	7,223	185	719
1991	7,280	180	560

Source: Andersson, P. & M. Ndulo, *Hyperinflation, Stabilisation, and the New Economic Recovery Program*, Mimeo. Department of Economics. University of Gothenburg, 1994, p.24.

Since 1970, Zambia's indebtedness has grown rapidly. In 1991 it stood at US$ 7.3 billion. This was equal to 560% of the country's export earnings and about 180% of GDP. External debt service payments, excluding arrears, in 1991 were equal to about 60% of her exports. For 1993, the picture remained largely unchanged. The debt service flow of US$ 391 million, or 44% of exports, alone absorbed 79% of the balance of payment support provided by donors. Presently, 70% of Zambia's debt is with multilateral agencies.

Debt servicing implies both a perverse resource transfer and a constraint on the import capacity. Because of its weighty debt burden, Zambia has to reduce both its recurrent and capital expenditures while interest payments have to be paid out of current exports and production. Furthermore, the import capacity is being constrained, a phenomenon that has created difficulties for the country's import-intensive manufacturing industry.

With respect to Zambia's monetary policies, the country has exercised strict controls over the exchange rate. It was not until 1990 that the Kwacha

[28] World Bank, ibid., p. 27.

was more or less set free to find its "true" market value. The development of the value of the Kwacha against the dollar is shown in Figure 3.4.

Figure 3.4. *The average nominal exchange rate 1980–1992*

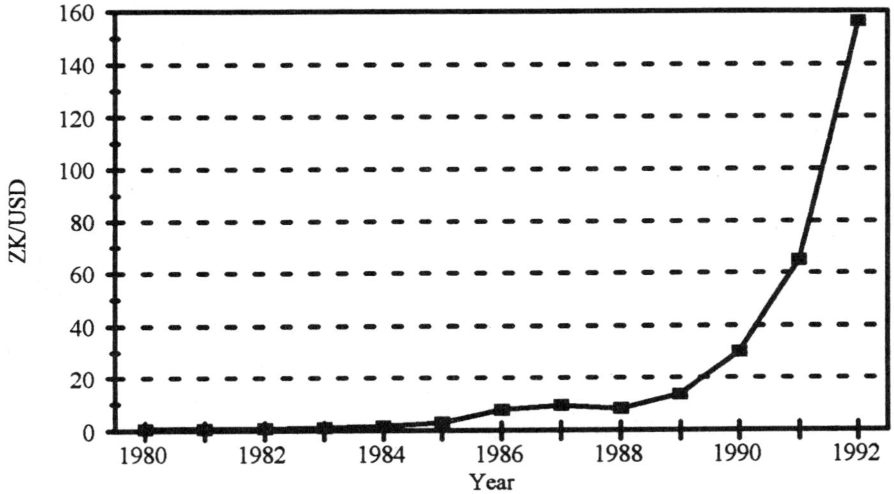

Source: Andersson, P. & M. Ndulo, *Hyperinflation, Stabilisation, and the New Economic Recovery Program*, Mimeo. Department of Economics. University of Gothenburg, 1994, p. 6.

The Kwacha has been continually falling in value since 1986. Since its regulation, it has fluctuated wildly. During the first 9 months of 1993, for example, it fell from K495.84 to the SDR in January to K747.51 in July. Thereafter, it appreciated up K610.09 in September. This had, however, less to do with any improvements in the economy but was more a function of a set of other factors such as: "asset switching"; the withdrawal of donor funds; copper price reduction; and lower import demand.[29] It is worth noting that the government introduction of high interest yielding treasury bonds resulted in asset switching from dollars to Kwacha. The demand for foreign exchange was also low because the general economic decline had led to reduced import requirements.

Internal imbalances are also phenomenal in Zambia. The economy has suffered from classical imbalances such as a high inflation; huge budget deficits; and a distorted price structure. Much of the emphasis of the structural adjustment programme has been directed towards eliminating these imbalances and establishing a basis for a meaningful economic take-off. By 1992, the inflation growth rate reached 191.2% as opposed to 111.1% the previous year. The situation improved in 1993 when the inflation rate was recorded to be 138.3%. Largely due to the government's adherence to the

[29] Andersson, P. and M. Ndulo, 1994, op. cit., p. 7.

cash budget, the average inflation in 1994 was as low as 35.1%. Several factors explained the high inflation growth rate in Zambia during the pre-1994 period. Firstly, the high expansion rate of aggregate demand had superseded supply. The large government deficit; high wage settlement; and over supply of money all worked towards increasing the growth in demand.

OVERVIEW

During the last 15 years, Zambia's economic decline has evidently been one of the worst in Sub-Saharan Africa. Since 1985, the GDP per capita decline has accelerated. This has been coupled with an increase in unemployment; a decline in real wages; and a reduction in transfers from the state to the average household. Taken together, this suggests a worsening poverty situation as confirmed by the average standard of living that has been on the decline since the 1970s. It has been estimated, for example, that in 1991, 67% of all households were poor and 58% extremely poor. Moreover, 75% of rural and 36% of urban households were recorded as extremely poor.[30] Preliminary data for 1993 suggests that the evidence of poverty continues to grow.[31]

The government tried in a number of ways to stabilise the economy. One noteworthy phenomenon regarding Zambia's macroeconomic trends has been the continuous policy shifts from the controlled to the liberalised regime and vice versa, often within incredibly short periods of time. Zambia has gone through a series of significant policy shifts since it attained political independence from Britain in 1964. Figure 3.5 gives a chronology of the country's economic policy changes over the years.

A few comments on how the state attempted to cope with the country's economic distress can shed some more light on the ups-and-downs of Zambian economic policies. Beginning with the Kaunda period (1964–91), the government's policy responses to the economic problems were both inadequate and, quite often, inadmissible. When the government was faced with reduced foreign exchange earnings following the collapse of the copper price on the world market, it erected a control regime and borrowed quite heavily from abroad under the wrong assumption that the crisis was temporary. Considering that Zambia at the time was classified as a medium income country, it managed to access multilateral institutions' resources on non-concessional terms. The country, thus, borrowed heavily to maintain its public consumption. Indeed, faced with declining domestic revenue, the country resorted to external borrowing to finance both the fiscal and current account deficit that stood at around 10% of GDP during much of the 1974–85 period. This explains how, by 1984, Zambia became the most indebted country in the world relative to its GDP.

---

[30] World Bank, 1993, p. 64.

[31] World Bank, 1994, p. 2.

Figure 3.5. *Chronology of Zambia's economic policy changes*

Period	Economic Regime
From independence to December 1982	Centralised planning and controlled regime
December 1982–October 1985	Decontrols and deregulation
October 1985–April 1987	Highly liberalised regime
May 1987–November 1988	Return to controlled regime
November 1988–June 1989	Relaxation of some controls
July 1989–April 1991	Return to highly flexible regime with movement towards full-scale liberalisation
May 1991–October 1991	Political transition with both government and the opposition expressing support for economic liberalisation
31 October 1991	New government of President Chiluba took over power from the old government of President Kaunda through elections
November 1991–Present	Fully-fledged Structural Adjustment Programme (SAP) and stabilisation policies

Another negative policy response was the government's decision to expropriate the assets of private companies under its policy of nationalisation. Consequently, there emerged in Zambia a proliferation of state-owned enterprises (parastatals) that operated within a sheltered market and which enjoyed a wide range of preferences, including privileged access to state subsidies and scarce foreign exchange; subsidised credit; guaranteed market; preferential tax concessions; and special treatment in their access to import licences.

It is evident from the above analysis that the pre-structural adjustment period in Zambia was characterised by a policy environment in which competition was restricted while industrial growth was largely based on import-substituting activity that operated behind high tariff walls. The high degree of protection and the consequent absence of competition, later reinforced by decreased capacity utilisation in industry, had led to decreased efficiency and escalated cost structure. Similarly, the policy of price control seriously affected corporate performance and profitability. In so far as the policy of price control had a high propensity to discourage efficient business operational ethics, this inhibited both new investments and the ability and willingness to finance plant maintenance. From the point of view of the manufacturing sector, price control in Zambia and the resultant enterprise inefficiency had tended to place supply at a much lower level than effective demand.

In order to cope with poor economic performance and failed economic responses, the government began in 1982 to stabilise the economy. Although a number of stabilisation packages were agreed with the IMF prior to the 1980s, most of these were aimed at demand management and hardly amounted to a comprehensive structural adjustment package. It was really the with 1983–85 package between the government and the IMF/World Bank that a comprehensive approach was tried. The programme covered a much wider range of structural policies. The components of the programme included a call for export diversification through an active foreign exchange policy, including devaluation; the introduction of the auction system in 1985, replacing the crawling exchange rate system; the abolishment of quantitative import restrictions; the decontrol of prices; a wage freeze; and restrictions on government expenditure in order to arrest the huge budget deficit.

What largely influenced the principal policy shifts that took place during the 1980s?

Beginning with the first major policy shift in May 1987 from the adjustment programme to a controlled regime, a number of factors are worth noting. During the post-1985 period and following a significant depreciation of the Kwacha; a rise in annualised rate of inflation; and the increase in consumer prices, pressure on the government to abandon the structural adjustment programme, in general, and the auction system, in particular, was, thus, mounted particularly by the strong organised labour. The political discontent that escalated against the programme burst out in food riots in December 1986 resulting in the loss of several lives and the auction of foreign exchange in particular was blamed for this. Political support for the entire IMF/World Bank structural adjustment programme was evidently lost especially amongst the average wage earners and the unemployed. Consequently, the government unilaterally abandoned the reform programme in May 1987 and returned to the controlled regime under its own New Economic Recovery Programme (NERP). Under NERP, the government re-activated import controls; limited debt service payments to only 10% of the net export receipts after the foreign exchange required to meet the needs of strategic sectors had been deducted; re-introduced price controls; returned to the system of interest rates being fixed by the government; re-introduced administrative allocation of foreign exchange; and revalued the Zambian currency.

Despite the government's decision to abandon the structural adjustment programme, its replacement, NERP, fared quite badly. As earlier demonstrated, the inflation growth rate continued to grow, consumer prices continued to rise, and money supply during the same period increased. Perhaps more importantly given the theme of this report, almost all the donor agencies decided to starve the country of the much sought out external assistance.

After mid-1988, the government recognised that economic dictates pointed to the need to return to the IMF and the World Bank's reform programme and it decided to gradually liberalise the economy. In June 1989, a comprehensive list of decontrol measures was put in place by the government, evidently in preparation for a smooth return to a highly flexible regime with movement towards full-scale liberalisation. Effectively, another U-turn being made and an economic and financial Policy Framework Paper, covering the 1989–93 period, was prepared by the government with assistance from the IMF and the World Bank. However, the political wind of change that increasingly called for the end to one party rule, compounded by the country's economic adversity, swept Kaunda out of office and a new government took over the reins of power after multi-party elections in October 1991. The new government committed itself to adopting the structural adjustment programme and in spite of the earlier presented economic difficulties emanating from the supposedly short-term adverse effects of the austerity measures adopted, no evidence up to now suggests that the government will moderate its commitment to the reform programme. In the financial sector, the new government freed the interest rates in September 1992 and liberalised the treasury bills market in January 1993. This was followed later by the decision to remove foreign exchange controls.

Considering the magnitude of the economic problems that have characterised the Zambian scene since 1974 when the economy began to experience serious resource constraints, it has not been surprising that the role of aid in the country assumed strategic significance. Faced with serious financial shortfalls and weak institutional capacities to support its developmental programmes, the government has continued to look to the donor community to provide external support. The nature, pattern, and magnitude of aid flows to Zambia are the subject of the next chapter.

Chapter 4

Aid Flows to Zambia

INTRODUCTION

A number of factors, both internal and external (see Chapter 3), combined to cause Zambia to solicit for increased externally-generated development assistance particularly after 1974. The aim of this chapter is to reveal the magnitude and pattern of external assistance to Zambia over the years. The major donors to the country are identified and the factors that influence the timing and volume of their flows to Zambia are examined. Like the previous one, this chapter adds to the organisational and economic framework within which aid is received and administered in Zambia .

AID FLOWS

Since the 1960s aid flows to Zambia have increased slowly, but steadily. A major leap was taken in the years 1977–79, and another significant increase took place in 1991. Figure 4.1 which provides the net aid to Zambia at constant 1992 prices over the 1961–1991 period confirms this reality.

Given the dismal performance of the Zambian economy, these flows also indicate an increased dependency on ODA. Both net ODA per capita and as a % of GDP has increased substantially. Average net ODA per capita, in current prices, for the years 1971–74 was $8. It had increased by almost ten times—$81—in the period 1989–1993. A similar trend was experienced for net aid as a proportion of GDP. In 1971–74 it was 1.8%, and by 1989–93 the average had increased to 18.2%.[32]

It is noteworthy that bilateral assistance has been much more significant in external resource flows to Zambia than multilateral aid. Among bilateral donors, the United Kingdom provided around 25% of total bilateral aid receipts during the 1970s, making it the major bilateral donor during that period. The United States and Sweden followed with 15% and 13% contributions, respectively. Zambia's other main bilateral donors during the 1970s were West Germany, Japan, Canada and Norway. The ranking of these countries in terms of their importance during the 1980s changed. Over the 1980–1991 period, it was Japan, followed by Germany then Sweden that constituted the major bilateral donors with respective contributions of 14%,

---

32 Adam, C., et al., 1994, p. 89.

13% and 12% of total receipts from bilateral sources. The Netherlands joined the list of Zambia's main bilateral donors during the 1980s and 1990s.

Figure 4.1. *Net bilateral and multilateral aid to Zambia, 1961–1991*

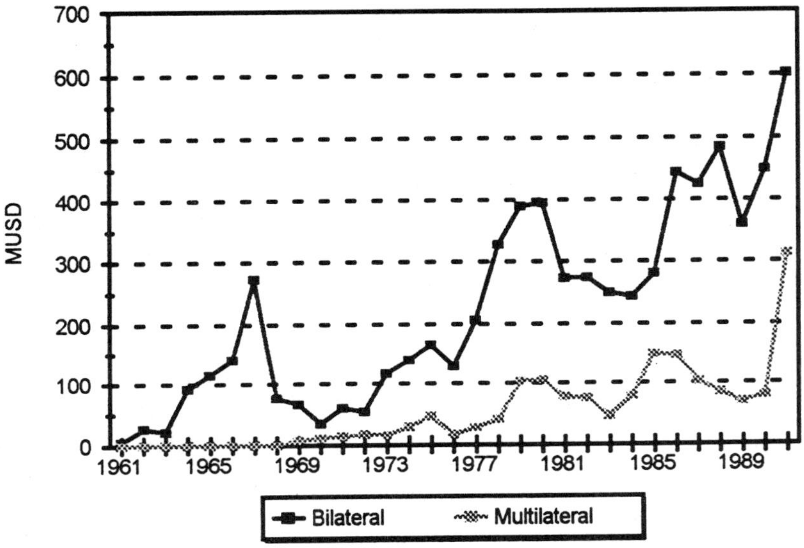

Note: The data have been deflated by the USA GNP deflator.
Source: OECD (Organisation of Economic Cooperation and Development), *Geographical Distribution of Financial Flows to Developing Countries*, various issue.

Apart from ODA, Zambia also received other resource transfers. These flows include official export credits, official sector equity and portfolio investment, and debt reorganisation undertaken by the official sector at non-concessional terms. In the DAC statistics they are classified as "Other Official Flows (OOF)". Net OOF generally gave a positive contribution during the period 1988–1991. The exception was 1991 when there was a net outflow of US$ 145 million, attributable to a negative transfer to multilateral agencies of US$ 178.2 million. Generally, for the whole period there was a negative resource transfer from Zambia to multilateral sources. However, this total hides differences between various multilateral agencies. In 1991, for example, the outflow of 178.2 was largely explained by the transfer to the World Bank of US$ 168 million. The IMF, IFC and the AFDB are other agencies with, at times, negative resource transfers of OOF to Zambia. As in the case of ODA, OOF from bilateral sources was more stable.

Private sector flows are usually not very important for most countries in southern and eastern Africa. Zambia is no exception. The OECD statistics use the following sub-categories: direct investments, portfolio investments and export credits. The total net contribution from these flows over the 1988–1991 period was US$ 143.3 million. Export credits and direct investments accounted for around 90% of private sector flows. Table 4.1 shows total external flows (i.e. aid and other flows) to Zambia over the 1988–1991 period.

Table 4.1. *Total external flows to Zambia, 1988–1991*

(US$ million)	1988	1989	1990	1991
Net ODA by DAC countries	407.4	314.2	408.9	582.8
Net ODA by multilateral agencies	70.8	60.0	72.0	301.4
Net ODA from all sources	478.2	374.2	480.9	884.1
Net OOF by DAC countries	12.4	19.6	47.2	33.1
Net OOF by multilateral agencies	34.3	16.2	18.8	-178.2
Net OOF from all sources	46.8	35.8	66.0	-145.0
Direct investments	0.9	37.6	-9.4	-0.3
Portfolio investments	-0.5	0.1	19.3	-6.8
Export credits	40.9	121.6	-16	37.9
Net private sector flows	-40.5	159.2	-6.2	30.8
Total external flows	484.5	569.2	540.7	769.9

Source: OECD (Organisation of Economic Cooperation and Development), *Geographical Distribution of Financial Flows to Developing Countries*, 1988/1991. Paris, 1993, pp. 296–297.

An equally noteworthy phenomenon in Zambia is the ever increasing importance of grants in total external assistance. With the exception of the 1978 to 1982 period and during 1991, external assistance to Zambia in the form of grants has been more significant than loans, an aspect that is evidently explained by the earlier demonstrated worsening debt crisis that persuaded the bilateral donors to extend their assistance chiefly in the form of grants.

Table 4.2 confirms the growing significance of the grant element in external assistance to Zambia for both bilateral and multilateral categories. With the exception of 1991, the grant element was almost 100% for bilateral and roughly 90% for multilateral assistance.

Table 4.2. *Grant element of external assistance to Zambia, 1988–1991* (%)

	1988	1989	1990	1991
Bilateral	94.6	97.2	99.1	69.7
Multilateral	92.7	89.6	96.8	84.4
Total	94.3	95.5	98.8	74.0

Source: OECD, *Geographical Distribution of Financial Flows to Developing Countries*, various issues.

In terms of the sectoral distribution of external support to Zambia, it is observable that agriculture, infrastructure, health and education received most of Western bilateral aid during the 1970s and 1980s. However, one observes that external assistance to the agricultural sector declined during much of the 1980s. Table 4.3 gives the percentage sectoral distribution of external assistance to Zambia over the 1985 to 1991 period.

Table 4.3. *Percentage distribution of aid flows to Zambia by sector, 1970–1991*

	1970–75	1976–80	1981–85	1986–91
Long-term inflows				
Social services	3.3	4.1	4.9	1.4
Infrastructure	38.0	21.6	18.6	21.2
Productive sectors	22.2	20.3	36.6	40.2
BOP support	0.0	29.6	12.2	18.8
Other	36.6	24.5	27.6	18.3
ODF Commitments				
Social services	-	-	-	13.5
Infrastructure	-	-	-	11.8
Productive sectors	-	-	-	20.8
Technical assistance	-	-	-	20.0
Programme	-	-	-	11.5
Debt Reorganisation	-	-	-	114.8
Other	-	-	-	17.5

Source: OECD, *Geographical Distribution of Financial Flows to Developing Countries*, various issues.

More recent data on development aid to Zambia indicate substantial progress in terms of size of flows. For example, project and non-project aid to Zambia in 1992 stood at an all time high of US$ 1,121.88 million. Of this amount, 44% was directed towards balance of payments support; 33% for project financing; 14% went to drought relief; and 10% to commodity aid. For 1993, external donors pledged a total of US$ 843.5 million as aid to Zambia out of which 53% was for balance of payments support aimed at improving the flow of essential imports into the country. Project financing received 43% of the pledges. Table 4.4 gives the 1992 overseas development assistance to Zambia as well as the 1993 commitments.

What factors influence the volume of aid to Zambia? Generally speaking, the volume and composition of external assistance to Zambia has been conditioned, first and foremost, by the country's willingness to reform its economy and, secondly, by the degree of economic adversity. The pattern of aid flows correlates closely with the country's policy changes. For example, during the first four years of independence up to 1968, aid to Zambia maintained a steady and upward movement. When the government decided to expropriate foreign assets through its policy of nationalisation, however, a significant drop in external assistance was registered. The UK, in particular, lowered its assistance significantly. When the Zambian economy began in mid-1974 to experience serious external shocks caused mainly by the drop in the price of copper and the increase in the price of oil, the donors responded positively by increasing their aid flows to the country. Over the 1974 to 1980 period, for example, external assistance to Zambia increased threefold.

Table 4.4. *Disbursements of ODA in 1992 and commitments for 1993* (US$ million)

Items	1992	1993
I. Total project financing	373.76	380.66
1. Economic sectors	232.90	236.41
(i) Agriculture & Food	82.07	70.28
(ii) Industry & mining	49.54	79.52
(iii) Energy	15.16	12.71
(iv) Transport	55.52	60.35
(v) Communication	30.61	13.55
2. Social sectors	56.21	74.97
(i) Education	30.25	32.09
(ii) Health	17.71	23.20
(iii) Water supply & sanitation	8.25	19.61
3. Other	84.65	69.48
II. Balance of payment support	488.63	438.21
III. Debt relief	18.40	0.00
IV. Commodity aid	88.61	21.09
V. Drought relief	152.48	3.34
Grand Total	1121.88	843.50

Source: UNDP (United Nations Development Programme), *Development Cooperation: Zambia, 1992*. Lusaka: UNDP, 1993.

When the IMF embarked on structural adjustment programmes (SAP) world-wide in 1980, Zambia's failure to design and implement an acceptable reform package led to a noticeable reduction in external support particularly from the bilaterals. When the country adopted SAP over the 1983 to 1987 period, this was rewarded with an appreciable increase of external assistance. During that period, the number of aid agencies that were active in Zambia stood at around 150. As expected, when the Zambian government unilaterally decided to abandon the IMF/World Bank-supported SAP in May 1987, many donors reduced significantly their support to the country. Major donors like the United States, UK and Germany actually suspended their disbursements completely. In other words, during the period when there was an absence of real agreements with the major international financial institutions, bilateral donors also reduced or abandoned their commitments to the country. A look at the nature of inflows to Zambia during the time when the country cancelled SAP confirms that the overall grant element in external receipts actually declined. As confirmed in Table 4.5, all indicators (interest rate, maturity, and grace period) worsened during the 1988–90 period when SAP was rejected. Thus, during that period, the grant element declined from 46.7% to only 22.6%. As soon as Zambia U-turned and adopted SAP from 1991 onwards, the grant element increased by more than threefold to 76.2%.

Table 4.5. *Terms of long-term inflows* (simple averages)

	1985–87	1988–90	1991–92
Interest rate	4.3	6.9	1.0
Maturity	29.9	15.9	39.6
Grace Period	7.8	4.7	9.9
Grant element	46.7	22.6	76.2

Source: World Debt tables as quoted from White & Edstrand, 1994, p.45.

After the 1989 resumption of negotiations with the IMF and World Bank which resulted in the production of the economic and financial Policy Framework Paper (PFP) that was prepared by the government together with the two multilateral institutions, aid began to flow again and has been sustained thereafter. Following the introduction of a multi-party system in which the new government has pledged total commitment to SAP, bilateral donors have maintained increased net inflows to Zambia.

A recent study[33] used world trade tables to show four series in external assistance to Zambia, namely, gross aid inflows (excluding debt relief); net aid transfers (i.e. inflows minus amortisation and interest payments on previous aid disbursements); aid minus all debt service; and total net transfer. On the basis of this, the study arrived at the following conclusions:

- there is a strong correlation between gross and net aid transfers, thus, confirming the point made earlier that external aid flows to Zambia have been highly concessional in nature in the past three decades. The growth of debt service obligations, particularly in the mid-1980s, has been such that it could not be offset by aid flows alone. This suggests that the external resources generated through SAP have been insufficient to meet the country's debt service obligations;
- up until the mid-1980s, there was a significant gap between net transfers and aid less debt service requirements. Due to the current increase in the grant element of inflows, the two categories are quite close; and

33 White, H. & T. Edstrand, 1994.

— over the 1990 to 1994 period, net transfers have been positive, thus confirming that aid from external sources has increased and/or stabilised significantly.

While, in global terms, donors have tended to link the volume of their commitments to Zambia's policy reform measures, not all the countries have responded in the same way. Zambia's rocky relationship with the major donors can be categorised into five periods that coincide with both significant shifts in flows as well as the government's policy commitment to reforms. These are (a) 1980 to 1983 being the period before SAP proper; (b) 1983–1987 when SAP was adopted; (c) mid-1987 to 1989 when the government abandoned SAP; (d) 1990–1991 when liberalisation was re-adopted; and (e) 1992 to the present when full scale and accelerated SAP has been adopted. If one assumes that donors that strongly link aid to reforms are those whose flows increased over the 1983–87 period; declined during the 1987–89 period; and remained substantial from 1990 to today, then Sweden, UK, and the Netherlands fit this classification in the case of Zambia. At another level, Germany and Canada only moderately link their aid disbursements to structural reforms (i.e. their aid increased when SAP was adhered to but also allowed moderate flows even during the non-reform intermissions). There are also those donors whose support seems to be disbursed independently of the reforms, i.e. where aid continued to grow both during the reform periods and in between and where net flows have actually declined in the post-1991 period when SAP is being fully and religiously adopted. Among such donors are Japan, Norway and the European Union. The last category of donors are those whose aid volumes actually flowed in the opposite direction. The UNDP falls in this rather rare category. For example, UNDP aid to Zambia declined during the period when Zambia first experimented with SAP and increased when the bilaterals withdrew their support following the May 1987 government abandonment of SAP. Similarly, during the current period when the country has embarked on full scale implementation of SAP, UNDP flows have slackened. This suggests that UNDP has tended to fill the gap when many major donors, particularly bilaterals, abandon the country for failure to reform.

In conclusion, it is evident that Zambia has received substantial external assistance in the form of both concessional loans and grants. To what extent have these considerable net flows been effective in meeting the needs of the recipient country? The case studies in the forthcoming chapters will attempt to answer this question from the perspective of the individual project. However, programme aid, or balance of payments support, has become increasingly important in the composition of the Zambian aid portfolio. Before concluding this chapter, we shall try to explore the macroeconomic effects from this type of aid.

MACROECONOMIC EFFECTS FROM BALANCE OF PAYMENTS SUPPORT

Balance of payments (BOP) support consists of import support and debt relief. Under import support, foreign exchange is not always linked to a specific project while under debt relief, the donor payment is usually targeted at meeting the recipient's bilateral or multilateral debt obligations.[34] BOP support has accounted for more than half of total aid to Zambia during 1992 and 1993. The shift in donor preferences to this form of aid during the 1980s was due mainly to the worsening foreign exchange situation in many African countries. In Zambia, BOP support is used more for maintaining existing investments and less for the creation of new ones. Moreover, this form of support has been linked to the ongoing structural reform measures as part of the donor conditionalities. Additionally, the payments emanating from import support are expected to lessen the strain on the government budget through a reduced need for deficit financing. Table 4.6 shows the sources and utilisation pattern of foreign exchange in Zambia over the 1989 to 1993 period.

Table 4.6. *Sources and uses of foreign exchange, 1989–1993* (US$ million)

	1989	1990	1991	1992	1993
Uses of forex					
Imports	102	1084	952	1302	950
Debt service	354	75	767	679	544
Payment of arrears	0	25	171	216	153
Total	137	2098	1890	2197	1647
Sources of forex					
Exports	1410	1263	1085	1111	949
Aid	236	422	798	1070	820
Debt relief	0	725	293	551	359
Change in reserves	-130	11	30	-95	-71
Other items	-142	-323	-316	-440	-410
Total	1374	2098	1890	2197	1647
Memo item: Net inflow	-118	133	153	726	482

Source: Mwanawima, I. & H. White, *Swedish Balance of Payments Support to Zambia*. Final report. SIDA, February 1995, Table 4.2.

34 During the last couple of years Sida, and a unit under the Ministry of Foreign Affairs, SASDA, initiated a number of research studies into the theoretical and methodological possibilities of analysing the impact of balance of payments support. Zambia has been a key case for these studies. This section attempts to present a summary of the findings of these studies.

To allow for a more focused analysis of BOP support on Zambia's macro economic conditions, the analysis that follows will look at import support and debt relief separately.

THE EFFECTS OF IMPORT SUPPORT

The traditional justification of aid in the process of growth and development is that of providing the required capital to the "needy" recipient country. Domestic savings in the aid receiving country are assumed to be too low under conditions where capital in the form of foreign direct investments has not been sufficiently forthcoming to compensate for this. The low savings level is, thus, seen as the principal explanatory factor behind the need for external capital injection. The classical expression of this position is found in the Harrod-Domar model where economic growth is determined by savings and the capital intensity within different economic sectors.

Another variant of the gap-model emphasising the lack of foreign exchange to pay for the necessary imports of intermediate and investment goods was developed as a response to the worsening balance of payments crisis in many developing countries. Aid, in this context, is supposed to provide the needed foreign exchange. White uses this argument as his point of departure for assessing the macroeconomic effects of aid in Zambia.[35] However, his attempt to model the macroeconomic effects of aid is constrained by the difficulty of establishing a strong cause-effect relationships between aid and growth. Although data seem to be sufficient to produce clear indications of the effects of aid on the macroeconomic trends, the attribution of such changes to aid flows is usually not conclusive.

Is there the existence of a savings gap in Zambia? Historically there seems to be little evidence of this. For the whole period 1965–1991, it appears that domestic savings usually have been sufficient to cover investments. There is, however, a clearly falling trend as a result of efforts to maintain consumption levels in the face of a serious reduction in incomes. Regarding the foreign exchange constraint, it is observable from Table 3.6 that export earnings have, even in spite of the adverse developments of terms of trade, been high enough to pay for imports. As imports and investments are largely financed from domestic resources, one would not expect them to reflect changes in aid inflows. Actually, there seems to be an inverse relationship—imports have fallen as aid has risen.

Whites analysis shows no significant impact of aid on imports. The capacity to import, it would seem, is significantly influenced by export receipts and the terms of trade. Indeed, existing evidence suggests that falling export receipts from copper and terms of trade deterioration have been

[35] White, H., et al., 1994, p. 115.

translated into lower imports.[36] Consequently, it can be concluded that aid has not necessarily facilitated increased imports into Zambia—nor has it intended to do so. A large proportion of aid has been debt relief rather than import support. BOP support directed towards import activity was channelled mainly through the Open General License (OGL) system. In the case of Swedish aid that was routed through OGL, 60% of the funds went to production related activity; 20% for infrastructure; less than 10% for consumer goods; and about 5% went to health and education. It is noteworthy, however, that the Zambian economy's structural weaknesses discussed in Chapter 3 have worked against the potential of import support to have any meaningful effect on the productive sectors.

Given the strong correlation between export performance, import capacity, and investment levels, White discussed the extent to which aid has had an adverse impact on exports through the "Dutch disease effects". His econometric analysis shows no relationship between aid and the real exchange rate (which is supposed to appreciate as a result of the Dutch disease). One noteworthy aspect in the Zambian case is that copper exports are not particularly sensitive to changes in the real exchange rate as revenues and a large part of their costs are denominated in the more stable US dollars. Devaluations do, however, affect local production costs positively through falling real wages. This, in turn, stimulates increased profitability. Whether this would have any impact on output is debatable. Low quality deposits; low productivity; and inefficiencies in ZCCMs operations are equally important determinants of output and profitability levels. Non-traditional (i.e. non-copper) exports behave differently under these conditions since they are directly affected by changes in the real exchange rate. Real depreciation—raising the relative price of imports—does switch demand to domestic production. White concludes that if aid affects the real exchange rate, it is through this channel that the balance of trade would be influenced.

BOP support may affect money supply in three different ways. Firstly, there is the direct effect through the use of counterpart funds. Counterpart funds have been believed to have an inflationary impact since they are an increase in government expenditure—putting more money into circulation in return for goods and services. This, however, is not always true since the money comes from the public. Since the government first collects money and then hands it back, there is no effect on the money supply. But any discrepancy between the value of counterpart funds collected and the actual amount that is spent would have an effect on the money supply. If more is collected than spent, there would be a contractionary effect.

Secondly, BOP support has an impact on the government budget deficit. The countervalue policies of most donors to Zambia state that the funds

---

36 White, H. & T. Edstrand, 1994.

should be used mainly for reducing the need for deficit financing, and not be associated with incremental expenditures. The cash budget system means that the funds should not be used for items in the primary budget. But they can be used for payment of domestic debt. If the government uses the countervalue to finance expenditures it was planning to make anyhow, then the need for deficit financing goes down. In any case, the effect of BOP support on money supply is less a matter of how counterpart funds are used and more a function of the government's monetary and fiscal policies. In the Zambian case, counterpart funds have primarily reduced the government's resort to deficit finance.

The impact of counterpart funds on the money supply depends on their impact on the budget deficit and on reserves. If there is no incremental expenditure, no reduction in tax collection, and no accumulation of reserves, then there is a contractionary effect on base money to the value of the counterpart funds. If the funds are all spent and reserves increase by the amount of the aid, then the money supply increases by the value of the counterpart funds. In the Zambian case, the contribution of total net claims on government by Bank of Zambia to changes in base money have been quite small, so the role of counterpart funds is still less. On the other hand, growth of reserves has played a major role in the expansion of base money, though it is difficult to attribute a share of the reserve accumulation to the aid inflow. The main conclusion to draw is that there is no theoretically unambiguous impact of counterpart funds on the money supply.

THE EFFECTS OF DEBT RELIEF

The macro economic effects of debt relief bring out two specific issues. The first refers to whether the debt would have been paid in the absence of the debt relief. If the debt would not have been paid, then debt relief would not have directly contributed any new resources. An inflow on the capital or current account would immediately be offset by an equivalent outflow. If the recipient would have paid the debt, then debt relief is the same as free foreign exchange since the money that would have been used for debt servicing is now available for alternative uses. Secondly, there is the existence of debt overhang, i.e. investment is constrained by high levels of debt. This effect operates in several ways. There is the problem of establishing just exactly how burdensome the debt actually is. Changes in interest rates, exchange rates, terms of trade etc., all have an impact on the size of the debt and the effort it would take to repay it. A highly indebted country has a limited access to private international capital markets, hence having difficulties to obtain credits for investments. Besides, repayment obligations act as a tax on present and future income. The likelihood of meeting debt obligations is greater the lower these burdens are. Therefore, reducing the debt burden can be expected to have a stimulating effect on investments even if the debt burden itself does not necessarily provide any additional funds.

Debt relief is least likely to have an effect on the money supply. If the donor pays US$ 1 million in debt relief and there are a corresponding US$ 1 million of debt obligations, then there are no implications for domestic money. If the inflow exceeds the amount required, then the surplus may either be used to service domestic debt or retained until an external payment is required. In the former case, the foreign exchange is sold for Kwacha which are then returned to the public such that there is no net effect. In the latter case, the potential impact on money supply due to the increases in reserves is neutralised by the requirement that the government increase its surplus at the Bank of Zambia by a similar amount. Only if these systems are not properly applied might debt relief affect money supply. In 1993, as much as 75% of the government's budget was covered by donors. For 1995, it was estimated that 85% of the budget needed to come from donor resources. External private inflows are negligible and for 1995, the financing requirement from donors was US$ 2.1 billion, including debt obligations.

In conclusion, the role of aid in Zambia's economic development is quite far from that predicted by conventional theory. As White concluded, "essentially, Zambia used non-concessional monies to repay borrowing from private creditors and is now receiving grants and concessional funds to repay these non-concessional debts. Aid inflows have thus for the most part been a large scale debt rescheduling device, and helped with a gradual reduction in the debt. The Zambian economy is not currently able to pay debt service and is not likely to be able to do so for many years to come—unless a large part of the debt is written down."[37]

Against the above background, the role of aid in Zambia has been a rather circular phenomenon. Donors provide aid mainly to enable Zambia to repay its debt—the debt largely owed to the same countries and institutions that provide the aid.

CONCLUSIONS

The aim of this chapter and the one before it was to provide the necessary background to the analysis of aid effectiveness in Zambia. The volume of aid flows to Zambia from both bilateral and multilateral donors suggests that the country is among the developing states that have registered significant flows. Indeed, it is evident that grants continue to constitute a much larger share of resource flows while loans are increasingly being concluded on softer terms. This change in the nature of the aid flow to Zambia is largely a reflection of the country's increasing economic adversity and the donor

[37] White, H. & T. Edstrand, 1994, op. cit., p. 286.

community's readiness, particularly after the country's adoption of SAP, to assist the economy to stabilise. Notwithstanding this positive trend, this chapter has revealed that donor conditionalities have characterised the donor–recipient interface in Zambia, a phenomenon that has significantly conditioned the pattern and volume of aid flow to Zambia.

The implications of what has so far happened in the Zambia-donor interaction raises a number of questions regarding the impact on aid effectiveness.

- Firstly, to what extent has the nature of the aid relationship influenced the degree to which Zambia has realised its development goals vis-à-vis external support?
- Secondly, has the Zambian government been able to articulate a development strategy, specific enough to allow for the creation of a reasonable policy environment within which donor activities are accommodated?
- Thirdly, has the donor community made an effort to design mechanisms and organisational structures that would allow them not only to respond positively to the developmental demands of the recipient but also to achieve this within the institutional framework that is set by the government.
- Fourthly, has the question of project/programme sustainability been seriously considered in the donor–recipient relations?
- Finally, how much coordination takes place within the government system; between the donors and the government; and within the donor community itself?

These questions permeate our analyses of the four case studies. The extent to which each case will enable us to satisfactorily answer all the questions will vary. But taken together the evidence presented in all of them should take us a long way towards providing a good picture of the nature of the aid relationship, as well as the causational links between the aid relationship and aid effectiveness.

Chapter 5

Zambia Educational Materials Project

BACKGROUND

In the past two decades or so, almost all schools in Zambia have suffered a critical shortage of educational materials particularly at the primary school level. Pupils had to learn without the requisite books and other educational materials that cater for a decent study environment. In many cases, even teachers did not have the handbooks that are needed for effective teaching. This state of affairs had been worsened chiefly by the declining budgetary resources going to the basic education level (covering primary schools and the first two years of secondary education). With ever-increasing demand for school places in a country with a population growth rate of 3.2% per annum, the need for more educational materials escalated.

At the supply level, the limited ability of the local publishing and printing industry to provide the needed books, on the one hand, and the government's limited ability to pay for the few that were produced, on the other, combined to worsen an already desperate situation. The state's ability to fill the gap left by the local book industry by way of imported educational materials was also compromised by the scarcity of foreign exchange. Moreover, the capacity of the government to distribute educational materials throughout the country was affected by a weak logistical support system and rigid organisational structures. Consequently, the quality of learning was adversely affected.

Against the above background, discussions were held between the Zambian and the Finnish governments in the early 1980s to find ways of solving the problem of the shortage of educational materials in Zambian schools. It was then decided that a feasibility study should be carried out by representatives from

- the Ministry of Higher Education, Science and Technology;
- the Ministry of General Education, Youth and Sport;
- the Curriculum Development Centre (CDC);
- The Kenneth Kaunda Foundation (later renamed the Zambia Educational Publishing House); and
- FINNIDA.

The conclusions of the feasibility study led to the formation of the Zambia Educational Materials Project (ZEMP) which was established in 1984 by the Finnish and Zambian government authorities with the overall objective of improving the supply and quality of school books in Zambia.

The first phase of ZEMP covered the 1984 to 1987 period and had as its main objectives the promotion of local capacity to develop, produce and distribute school books and, as an emergency measure, to reprint a number of titles that already existed. This initial phase of the project was evaluated in mid-1987 and on the basis of the recommendations and government reactions thereon, Phase II, covering the 1988–91 period, was initiated. The objectives of Phase II of ZEMP were listed as follows:

— development of the quality of locally-generated school materials (long-term objective);

— development of the capacity for local production of educational materials (long-term objective);

— rehabilitation of the quality of primary education (short-term objective); and

— development of self-sufficiency and minimisation of costs of provision of educational materials.

Phase II was evaluated in early 1991 and Phase III, covering the 1991—94 period, was initiated with the following objectives:

— development of the quality and relevance of education through the provision of educational materials;

— supply of educational books to primary and secondary schools in priority subjects (mainly science, mathematics and English);

— improvement of writing of educational books through strengthening the capacity of the Curriculum Development Centre (CDC) and publishers; and

— improvement of local publishing, printing and distribution capacity to meet the needs of primary and secondary education.

PROJECT FINANCING

ZEMP is chiefly financed by FINNIDA and, in principal, the project manages only funds donated by this donor agency. The actual disbursement of FINNIDA funds under ZEMP is handled by the Project Coordinator (see below). The significant role of the Swedish International Development Authority (SIDA) in ZEMP activities is noteworthy. SIDA's educational materials sub-programme, under its Educational Sector Support Programme, has been running since 1985. Under this sub-programme, the Zambian government's Ministry of Education receives financial support that facilitates the acquisition and distribution of educational materials to all basic education schools run by the government. Over the years, SIDA, through this subprogramme, has provided textbooks, exercise books, teachers' guides, wall maps, braille materials and supplementary materials. A particularly noteworthy aspect here is that the SIDA activities have been coordinated with FINNIDA-funded ZEMP. In the arrangement, SIDA funds are used, through ZEMP, for the production of textbooks. With the Educational Materials Unit (EMU) that was created in 1990 under the Ministry of Education (see below), SIDA funds were being channelled through this unit whose director was responsible for the use of these resources.

Other donors are involved, at a much lower level, in ZEMP support. First, NORAD has provided equipment to ZEPH through import support. Second, since 1982, the ODA/British Council has continued to support the positions of English language specialists at CDC. Third, the Zambian government contributes but very marginally to ZEMP.

ZEMP ORGANISATIONAL FRAMEWORK

Zambian Educational Materials Coordinating Committee

Immediately ZEMP was established in 1984, the ministry responsible for education constituted a committee that was mandated to monitor the activities of the project. It was called the Zambia Educational Materials Project Coordinating Committee (ZEMPCC). Initially, this Committee handled only the activities of ZEMP. With the emergence of wide-ranging issues in the provision of education materials, ZEMPCC was reconstituted to become an all-embracing Zambia Educational Materials Coordinating Committee (ZEMCC) and was assigned the following terms of reference:

- to formulate educational materials policy for the consideration of the appropriate decision-makers;
- to establish the level of national need for educational materials and propose how such needs could be met;
- to propose how the required resources could be mobilised to support identified needs;
- to review and monitor the progress of projects that deal with the supply of educational materials;
- to coordinate donor support for educational materials provision; and
- to address specific implementation issues, deadlines and constraints to improved delivery of educational materials.

Under the chairmanship of the Ministry of Education's Assistant Secretary (Technical Assistance), ZEMCC reports to the Permanent Secretary of the Ministry of Education while its membership includes representatives from the ministry itself; the National Commission for Development Planning (NCDP), Kenneth Kaunda Foundation, now Zambia Educational Publishing House (ZEPH); and the donor community.

Opifer Limited

A Finnish consulting firm, Opifer Ltd, was sub-contracted by FINNIDA to be ZEMP activities' executing agency and was assigned the following tasks:

— general project supervision and support;

— procurement of goods in liaison with FINNIDA and the Finnish Government Procurement Office (VHK); and

— recruitment of expatriate personnel and handling of staff matters.

Through its Lusaka-based expatriate Project Coordinator, Opifer coordinates ZEMP's various components. The Project Coordinator also administers the project budget which includes updates, revisions, and local disbursements. The coordinator, additionally, handles ZEMP planning and implementation issues.

Opifer recruited a good number of expatriate advisers, apart from the Project Coordinator. These were the production adviser; two editorial advisers; research adviser, distribution adviser; and the engineer. Even the Project Secretary was an expatriate. As of December 1992, there were no local personnel employed directly by ZEMP except the project driver and the book keeper. At the same time, 90 local teachers were seconded to the project through CDC and served as part-time writers while all full-time indigenous posts were phased out.

Educational Materials Unit

In recognition of the growing concern that ZEMP was not adequately integrated into the government system and, thus, perceived to have operated outside the state institutional framework (see below), the Educational Materials Unit (EMU) was established in 1990. In principle, ZEMP was expected to discharge its functions under this unit. EMU served as the secretariat of ZEMCC and it represented the Ministry of Education on a broad spectrum of educational materials issues. The Director of EMU was answerable to ZEMCC as well as to the Permanent Secretary of the Ministry of Education through the Assistant Secretary in charge of technical assistance.

Although the Unit was established in 1990, its director was only appointed in July 1993. By the end of 1993, the director's functions were expanded to include the general procurement functions of the Ministry of Education. This resulted in the overloading of the EMU director who, consequently, had less time for activities related to educational materials functions.

Similarly, since the Unit was inadequately staffed, ZEMP expatriate advisers had to perform tasks that were outside the scope of their assignments.

The Ministry of Education Procurement and Supplies Unit (MEPSU) was established in January 1994 and, through a ministerial decision, EMU would cease to exist and its activities that were related to educational materials would be performed by the Education Materials Section (EMS) of MEPSU. It was also decided that the director of EMU would become director of MEPSU.

At the actual operational level, ZEMP support to educational materials provision is handled at a number of levels. Firstly, on the *supply* side, ZEMP extends its assistance mainly through its institutional support to the state-owned Zambia Educational Publishing House (formerly KKF); and to the CDC.

Zambia Educational Publishing House (ZEPH)

The support of ZEPH is founded on ZEMP's overall objective of strengthening the local capacity for the publication of the required educational materials. ZEPH was singled out as worth supporting chiefly because, with the then emphasis on state-run and financed educational provision, it was the only government-run educational organisation that qualified for support. ZEPH was, thus, ear-marked for expansion and improvement at both the publishing and printing levels through, *inter alia*, the provision of machinery, technical advice, and training. At present, ZEPH's total machine capacity is accounted for by FINNIDA/ZEMP as well as NORAD donations. At the *distribution* level, ZEPH receives the following support from ZEMP:

- a distribution adviser for guidance on marketing and distributional logistics;
- vehicle and equipment to assist in distribution; and
- vehicles maintenance workshop.

Despite this support, it was discovered that many school books were not reaching schools in time. In an attempt to correct this problem, ZEMP, in conjunction with District Education Officers, has established Zonal Distribution Centres (ZDCs) where books are delivered and from where primary schools, in turn, are expected to collect their allocations. School books meant for secondary schools are delivered directly to their destinations.

Curriculum Development Centre (CDC)

ZEMP support to the improvement in the quality of locally-produced school materials (in terms of their content and design) has also been channelled through CDC. The Center is in charge of the development of primary and secondary school curriculum although the Examinations Council of Zambia is ultimately in charge of the approval of such curriculum. ZEMP has donated data- and word-processing facilities to CDC in order to improve the quality of the materials produced. ZEMP also supports the development of new textbooks at CDC through, *inter alia*, (a) the support for two editorial advisers and (b) financing of writing workshops. ZEMP has also provided on-the-job training in planning and writing educational materials. The main aim of this exercise is to create a pool of trained local writers, particularly in mathematics and science fields.

PROJECT IMPLEMENTATION

General issues

It is important to state at the outset that the analysis of ZEMP performance below covers the period up to the end of 1993 and is based mainly on the project evaluation reports made up to that period. The aim here is to demonstrate how the project organisation and management fared up to this point in time so as to allow for the drawing of conclusions and learning of lessons about aid effectiveness. Since the analysis covered mainly that period, little is said about the more recent initiatives that may suggest a different *modus operandi* and performance record.

ZEMP's overall objective has remained the same throughout its phases. It has really been at the implementation level that different approaches have been used largely in response to the economic climate in the country. Perhaps the most important change, though still in the process of being consolidated , has been the altered perspective regarding who should be the project's implementation partner. As demonstrated earlier, the major implementation partners of ZEMP have been ZEPH and CDC, both of which are government-owned. Under the old system, CDC developed the scripts (with the help of ZEMP advisers) which it then handed over to ZEPH that handled the publication and printing functions. After the book was published, the Ministry of Education bought the copies using SIDA-donated funds; then ZEPH arranged for their distribution (with the help of the ZEMP distribution adviser), again using SIDA funds.

Although under this system, individual authors and publishers were free to develop and publish educational materials, there was no guarantee that the Ministry of Education would buy them. Since the government's educational materials budget was eroded significantly by both inflation and limited financial allocations to the Ministry of Education, the market for materials from the 'private sector' was extremely limited. Consequently, ZEPH, under ZEMP support, had the monopoly not only of CDC's scripts but also of the larger part of the educational book market in Zambia.

Following the introduction of liberal economic policies, the government decided to free the educational publishing industry in Zambia, thus removing the monopoly of CDC and ZEPH not only in terms of school book supply but, more importantly, with respect to government-cum-donor support.

A look at the performance of ZEMP's first and second phases shows the following picture:

— over the 1985 to 1990 period, roughly 5.2 million ZEMP books were printed and distributed under the project;

— a further 2.3 million books were in the process of distribution at the beginning of 1991 and another 3.3 million books were at different processing stages.

The above figures show that by the end of Phase II of the project, approximately 69% of the targeted number of books were produced, thus, leaving a failure rate of 31%. Out of the 5.2 million books that were distributed, 5 million (or about 96%) went to primary schools while the remainder were for secondary schools.

Notwithstanding the above generally good record of performance, it is perhaps at the level of *text books* production and distribution (as opposed to exercise books) where major problems appear. For example, ZEMP produced and distributed only about 29% of its estimated target of textbooks in 1990 while in 1991, this stood at 49%. By the end of June 1992, the project supplied only about 300,000 textbooks, constituting roughly 18% of its estimated output that year.

Another important aspect of ZEMP implementation that has important implications for project effectiveness regards the roles of (a) the project Coordinator; (b) ZEMP expatriate advisers; (c) the FINNIDA office in Lusaka; and (d) Opifer, the Finnish company that was sub-contracted to implement ZEMP. With respect to the Project Coordinator, it is evident that there has been considerable overconcentration of power and authority in the hands of this official. As the project's phase two evaluation stated

> ... the project and its image might have been better served if there had been devolution of responsibilities to the counterpart and to other ZEMP personnel; if there had been a limit to the terms of the coordinator; and if major policy and strategy issues and matters affecting the budget had to a larger extent been referred to ZEMCC ... A further outcome of the concentration of all management tasks is that this had overloaded the coordinator with more work than he could reasonably be expected to shoulder ... An important outcome of this is that the project had been allowed to move from year to year without any significant readjustment in its priorities or strategies.[38]

Secondly, with respect to the role of ZEMP advisers, the ZEMP organisational structure was constituted in such a way that they assumed an important role. Their input has generally been positive. A few examples of this perfor-

[38] Kelly, M.J., et al., 1991, p. 59.

mance during Phase II of the project may confirm this general conclusion. For example, the Editorial Adviser in charge of mathematics and science has played a positive facilitative role in the project's development and publication of educational materials. Under his direction, ZEMP has provided considerable on-the-job training in the planning and writing of educational materials with a view to, *inter alia*, building a pool of trained indigenous writers. By the end of ZEMP's Phase II, 100 writers had benefited from this training. The Editorial Adviser also facilitated the introduction of word processing to both secretarial and professional staff at CDC. At ZEPH, the Editorial Adviser helped to set up procedures for the efficient flow of work within the editorial department, an input that is expected to equip local staff with a broader view of publishing. The Adviser also assisted in the acquisition of editing skills by local editors through, for example, editorial skills management courses/workshops that were mounted both within the country and in-house.

Moreover, the Distribution Adviser, another ZEMP-supported expert, was mandated to develop, in broad terms, the distributional capacity of ZEPH. In the short term, the Adviser was expected to provide, in reasonable time and at realistic cost, technical advice on the distribution of all educational titles to the nine regional depots/sales outlets; to 55 District Education Officers' offices; and to 328 Zonal Distribution Centres. Thus, the Adviser's major task was to overhaul ZEPH's distributional set-up through better planning routines. Generally, the District Adviser provided guidance and advice to ZEPH's marketing department on aspects related to distribution and logistics, especially with regard to the setting up of a zonal distributional system. With the help of the Distribution Adviser, the old system whereby KKF distributed ZEMP books to its regional warehouses for onward transmission to the District Education Officers was replaced by a new improved system in which a number of sub-centres have been established at various schools in each district. Schools within easy reach of the sub-centre draw their supplies from there. In the 55 districts in the country, a total of 3,458 schools were served as of 1991 and they drew their supplies from 354 sub-centres.

Despite the positive efforts of the Distribution Adviser, the performance of the ZEMP book distribution system has been found to be weak. According to the end-of-contract report of the Distribution Adviser, as of December 1992, "only about 30% of the distributed books went according to plan to sub-centres. Meanwhile, the rest (70%) were first dumped [at] District Education Officers' offices which are not easily accessible."[39] According to the mid-1993 *Quarterly Report* of ZEMP, the situation had not changed much:

---

[39] Seppala, J., 1992.

> The distribution of textbooks by ZEPH is facing serious problems ... The deliveries from the central warehouse progressed fairly well ... but ... regional offices have not enough working capital to run the distribution system as planned. Plenty of books have been found at regional warehouses and the delivery time within the region of 4–5 months.[40]

The major reason for this, according to regional managers, is that after paying for salaries and related expenses, the system is usually left with very little money to handle the distribution function. The poor mechanical state of the distribution trucks further affected the efficient distribution of educational materials to schools.

ROLE OF *FINNIDA* OFFICE AND *OPIFER*

With respect to the role of the FINNIDA Office, the ZEMP Phase II evaluation report revealed that the Development Office in the Finnish Embassy seemed to lack a good picture of the ZEMP project issues. Although this could partially be explained by the Development Office's inadequate staffing, thus making it not easy for the embassy to closely monitor the activities of ZEMP, it is highly probable that the vagueness of the project's objectives (see below) and the absence of clear organisational guidelines contributed to the low level of the donor agency's direct input at the project implementation level. The overcentralisation of the project tasks in the hands of Opifer's appointed Project Coordinator further contributed to the low level of involvement of the FINNIDA office in Lusaka. In fact, as the end of Phase II project evaluation report observed, "the division of responsibilities between the project in Lusaka; the Opifer office in Helsinki; the Development Office in the Lusaka embassy; and the FINNIDA desk in the Ministry of Foreign Affairs in Helsinki appears not to be clear to all persons involved with the project".[41]

Consequently, the supervisory role of FINNIDA and the home office of Opifer had been significantly smaller than is usually the case even when a private consultant is sub-contracted to extend the services.

With respect to the role of Opifer Limited, it is clear that, in principle, there are advantages in contracting a private firm to implement a project since such an arrangement reduces the donor's administrative workload. The tasks involving the recruitment of experts; maintaining contracts with suppliers of equipment and related machinery and spare parts etc. are usually better handled by a specialised private company. The only disadvantage of this arrangement is that it requires closer monitoring by the donor to ensure that, while the system of operating purely on commercial principles has its advantages, this is not done at the expense of the much

---

[40] ZEMP, *Quarterly Report.* October–December 1993.

[41] Kelly, M.J., et al., 1991, op. cit., p. 60.

broader concerns of donor effectiveness that go beyond the economic and technical considerations of service provision to the more long-term aspects regarding, *inter alia*, project sustainability beyond the involvement of external support.

When looked at in the above broader context, ZEMP's management structure during the period under review was evidently *not* a good example of a success story. The role of Opifer in the global scheme of things was unclear even to some of the project advisers that it had recruited. The opinion of the Distribution Adviser, himself recruited by Opifer, is revealing:

> The role and functions of the Head Office—Opifer Ltd.—has been unclear ... and the service through them has usually been slow. Clear and approved procurement orders are usually stuck somewhere for several months before the order is actually placed. It is difficult to know who is more to blame, Opifer or VHK.[42]

Against the above analysis that attempted to highlight ZEMP's background; project financing; and organisational-cum-management framework roughly up to the end of Phase II of the project, the last part of this case study looks at the project's effectiveness and sustainability from the recipient perspective.

ZEMP EFFECTIVENESS AND SUSTAINABILITY

ZEMP's effectiveness up to 1993 is analysed below in the context of, firstly, project identification and design, particularly with respect to who conceived the project and the degree to which the project objectives allowed for both the ease with which it could be administered and the realisation of the government's stated goals or expectations from the project. Secondly, a closer examination of the project sustainability is made paying particular attention to issues regarding the development of indigenous human resources; the dependability of the project's organisational framework; and the sustainability of physical (including financial) resources needed for project survival.

PROJECT IDENTIFICATION AND DESIGN

Firstly, as earlier demonstrated, the establishment of ZEMP was a product of a joint effort between the Zambian government and the donor agencies, particularly FINNIDA. Upon the recognition of the gravity of the educational materials crisis in schools, the Zambian government held negotiations with the Finnish authorities regarding how the problem could be solved. As shown earlier, the feasibility study that was undertaken included representatives from both the Zambian government and FINNIDA. In this respect, it

---

[42] Seppala, 1992, op. cit., VHK is the Finnish Government Purchasing Centre.

is evidently clear that the conceptualisation of ZEMP involved principally the Zambian government.

Notwithstanding the fact that the ZEMP identification and design was a collective effort, it is noteworthy that serious flaws can be identified regarding the formulation of the project objectives/goals, a phenomenon that has adversely affected the effectiveness of the project's implementation. ZEMP's objectives, particularly during its first two phases, were too broad and all-embracing and obviously paid little attention to the capacity of the implementation organs. A closer examination of the objectives of Phase II of the project, covering the 1988–91 period, has revealed a number of weaknesses in both the objectives themselves and the project plan. One of these is the project's second objective, namely, the development of the capacity for local publication of educational materials, aimed at the enhancement of KKF's organisational capacity in the fields of editing, typesetting, printing, and binding. The distribution of educational materials was the principal strategy. The success indicators for this objective included the price and delivery times of ZEMP-financed books; stock levels of textbooks; and the cost and the production time of syllabi and guides. The main problem with this objective was that whereas it made an express reference to *publications*, the indicators used refer exclusively to printing and distribution instead. No mention what-so-ever of such publishing tasks as book development and financing is made, thus, creating an impression that wrong tools/indicators were being used to gauge the level to which this objective was being realised. A clear confusion between publishing and printing was obvious present at this level, a phenomenon that seriously compromised the process of determining the level to which this objective could be realised.

A further weakness occurs with respect to the project's third objective, i.e. the rehabilitation of the quality of primary education, it is clear that the scope of this objective was too broad for it included almost all that is required in the rehabilitation of primary schools, including buildings. And yet what was intended to be covered by ZEMP under this objective was the enhancement of primary educational quality through adequate supply of textbooks. It is also surprising that no reference was made regarding the need for book imports considering the low capacity of the printing industry at the time. To assume, as the project plan's objective and its indicators suggested, that all books would be produced within the country was not only too ambitious but clearly overestimated the capacity, real and potential, of the fragile local publishing industry.

Against the above background, one observes that not only were some of the project objectives unclear and, in some cases vague but, equally important, the connection between the stated objectives and the proposed measures (i.e. strategies to realise the objectives) was not always logical. Consequently, it can be concluded that the poor formulation of some of the ZEMP objectives; the manner in which these were interpreted; and some of the indices that were employed to monitor the realisation of these objectives all introduced serious difficulties in the implementation and, hence, effectiveness of the project. The absence, in a few cases of logical connections between the objectives and the strategies needed for their realisation also suggested rather hasty project design work.

INDIGENOUS HUMAN RESOURCES

Generally speaking, ZEMP has provided an extensive training programme which, at the end of Phase II of the project, accounted for 10% of the total budget for that phase. Much of this training, covering formal and in-house programmes and targeted at CDC writers, curriculum developers, editors, designers, and graphic artists has had a direct bearing on the realisation of ZEMP's objective of developing and consolidating Zambia's capacity to produce educational books. Training in book editing, printing, data processing and distribution was also extended to indigenous people at CDC and KKF. Hence, even though the number of books that were developed and produced by ZEMP may be small relative to planned targets, the lasting impact of the training component should be the quality of the country's educational materials. However, such other considerations as the ability of publishing institutions (e.g. ZEPH) to retain skilled manpower do seriously compromise the extent of benefits to be derived from ZEMP's training programme.

Notwithstanding the positive achievements of ZEMP's human resource development component, a number of problems at this level threatened the sustainability of the project. First and foremost, there was evidence that the concept of local counterparts to the Project Coordinator and advisers had received scanty attention under ZEMP during the period up to 1993. Beginning at the level of the Project Coordinator, serious anomalies emerged regarding the manner in which the counterpart was appointed. The man who was seconded from ZEPH to serve as a counterpart to the ZEMP project Coordinator was later also appointed to serve, as a supplementary responsibility, as the Director of EMU. As observed earlier, EMU was created under the Ministry of Education to act as the overall government organ in charge of all educational materials and for *all* the government projects (including ZEMP) that operate in this area. In this regard, the ZEMP Project Coordinator was, in principle, accountable and answerable to the Director of EMU—who was, in this case, also his counterpart. The two responsibilities were obviously difficult to reconcile and this aspect tended to confuse the line of command particularly as to who, in the government system, the ZEMP Project Coordinator was answerable.

Equally significant and related to the above, the relationship between the Project Coordinator and his local counterpart has been rather confused. As the project's phase two evaluation indicated,

> ... although a counterpart to the Project Coordinator has been named, little progress has been made in entrusting him responsibility for the functions of the project. It appears that he participates in core project management and coordinating activities only in conjunction with the Coordinator, but never independently, even when the Coordinator is absent.[43]

With respect to the counterparts of advisers, again no indication of a comprehensive knowledge transfer programme from the expatriate to the local personnel is evident. A number of advisers, particularly the Editorial Adviser, had succeeded in facilitating the transfer of knowledge and skills to the system for improving the quality and quantity of educational materials. In so far as this is one of the objectives of ZEMP, it ought to be acknowledged as an achievement. However, it is at the level of empowering the counterparts with the administrative, planning and supervisory skills to sustain this achievement where some weaknesses were established in the Phase II evaluation. It is evident that Opifer's terms of reference did not possess an explicit mandate to ensure that, at the end of its assignment in Zambia, a well-established cadre of skilled personnel would be in existence to take over from them. The sequencing of the withdrawal of advisers also suggests this serious anomaly. The Editorial Adviser's sentiments in his end-of-contract report over his withdrawal from CDC is instructive in this regard:

> This is not in fact a good time for me to withdraw from CDC. At the time when [the other Editorial Adviser] and I proposed that from 1993 onwards there would not be need for both of us, we expected that by now... the editorial department could have been well established and the personnel trained. Neither of these things have in fact happened and I leave at a time when a substantial practical input would have been useful.[44]

What the above sentiments suggest is that after several years of serving as adviser with an assigned local counterpart, the Editorial Adviser still felt that the relevant personnel that should have been trained were still not trained to take over his functions.

Generally, the question of counterparts continued to threaten the project's sustainability. It would appear that the government remained contented with the tasks that were performed by expatriate personnel—as long as the donor was willing to finance these posts. For a long time, the planned local posts of officers responsible for publishing; production and distribution; and finance and administration were not appointed. Thus, the four ZEMP advisers had no counterparts. And yet, as the January–March 1993 *Quarterly Report* of ZEMP lamented, "the establishment of EMU and transfer from ZEMP advisers to their counterparts represents the main thrust of sustainability in Phase III of ZEMP".[45] In protest to what was being perceived

[43] Kelly, M.J., et al., 1991, op. cit.

[44] Evans, J., 1992, pp. 7–8.

[45] ZEMP, *Quarterly Report,* January–March 1993.

Figure 5.1. *Actors and relationships in the ZEMP*

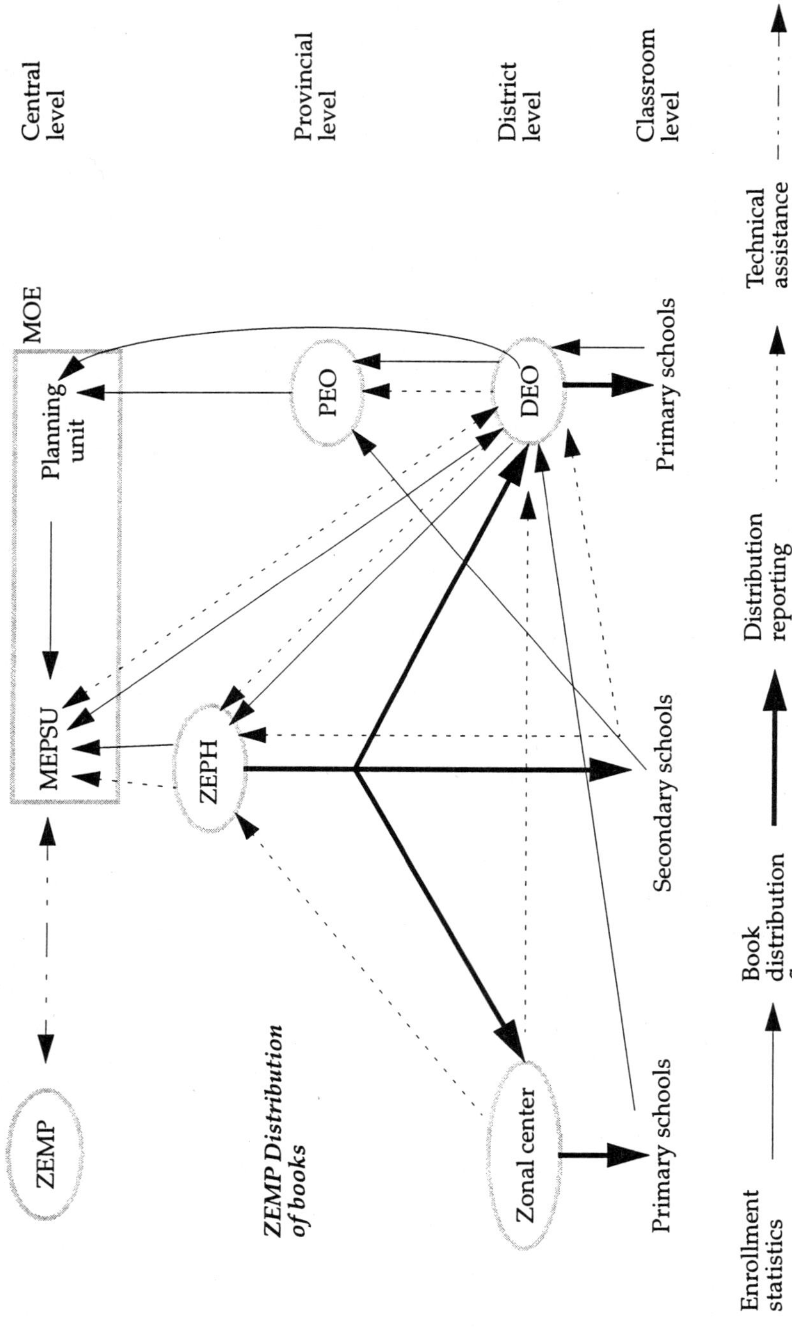

as lack of government commitment, FINNIDA stated during the December 1993 ESSP Supervisory Board meeting that "the Ministry of Education had not fulfilled the project agreement [terms] by not providing counterparts to ZEMP advisers and directed that ZEMP advisers suspend their work with EMU until the respective officers are appointed and on duty." FINNIDA further complained that "the delay in staffing EMU will make it almost impossible to fulfil the objectives related to the establishment of sustainable procurement systems at EMU".[46] From this, it can be concluded that the importance of counterparts was seen to be essential more by the donor than by the recipient. What this meant was that one year before FINNIDA technical and financial support was scheduled to end, the local counterpart personnel that were expected to ensure project sustainability were not appointed and in post.

ORGANISATIONAL FRAMEWORK AND RELATIONSHIPS

To fully appreciate the effectiveness of ZEMP, one needs to appreciate the functional relationships that exist at both the headquarters (i.e. between the donor agency in Lusaka; the Ministry of Education; and the role of central policy making structures at this level) and the local level (that include the provincial; district; and community or project levels). The analysis below attempts to reveal the nature of these relationships as they existed at least up to 1994. Figure 5.1 portrays the main actors and their relationships in the ZEMP project organisation.

Headquarters level

One major weakness of ZEMP was the earlier demonstrated absence of an explicit organisational framework or structure that would have facilitated a clear demarcation of responsibilities. The 1988–91 Project Plan, for example, was almost silent on ZEMP's organisational structure except for the statements to the effect that there would be a full-time coordinator who would serve as a liaison officer for all aspects of the project, including all financial matters. Further reference was made regarding the role of Opifer in the project's overall planning and monitoring and in the recruitment of external experts; handling financial arrangements with donors as well as arrangements for training. Beyond this, the project Plan was completely silent on the following important questions:

— ZEMP's relationship with the Ministry of Education in Zambia;

— the position and functions of the Project Coordinator's counterpart (apart from an incidental reference, in passing, in the plan's preface to the effect that the coordinator shall have a counterpart);

[46] ZEMP, *Quarterly Report*, October–December 1993.

— ZEMP's relationship with ZEMCC (and, consequently, with EMU). Although ZEMCC was identified as being responsible for overall planning, this, like in the case of the coordinator's counterpart, was only incidentally mentioned in the preface while in the main report the task of "overall planning and monitoring" was expressly assigned to the home office (i.e., Opifer in Helsinki);

— the roles of other ZEMP personnel in the activities of the project, apart from

— expatriate advisers; and

— the role of Opifer in relation to FINNIDA in both Zambia and Finland and to the Finnish Embassy in Lusaka.

As a result of the absence of clear specifications on the above important issues, difficulties in the various organ's operational relationships had persisted. More seriously, ZEMP's semi-independent management structure had tended to insulate it from not only the Zambian government's Ministry of Education but also from other institutions in the country that one would have expected the project to have had closer association with. The conclusion of the project's Phase II evaluation team endorsed this concern:

> ... the Project has tended to remain a foreign body within the Zambian and Ministry [of Education] context, isolated from the shocks and needs that press in on local institutions. ZEMP is greatly appreciated for its success in having textbooks developed, published, printed and distributed, but there is some uneasiness [in the country] about the way in which this success has been achieved. In particular, there is disquiet that more responsibility for the management and execution of the Project activities has not been devolved locally. [47]

The organisational structure of ZEMP at least up to 1993 further revealed another serious anomaly, namely, the lack of a decision-making body, an aspect that allowed the Finnish Project Coordinator to possess unlimited powers and be answerable to authorities outside the Zambian government system. This aspect is very evident when one takes a closer look at ZEMP's *modus operandi*. First, although the Coordinating Committee (ZEMCC) was expected to include policy formulation and project monitoring among its objectives (see above), it has been established that:

— the activities of ZEMCC were so broad that they covered *all* aspects and activities regarding educational materials and not only those pertaining to ZEMP. This had compromised the Committee's concentration on ZEMP policy and management issues;

— from the earlier-listed terms of reference of ZEMCC and its membership, it could not, for all intent and purpose, act as ZEMP's decision-

[47] Kelly, M.J., et al., 1991, op. cit., p. 57.

> making body. In fact, although the project organisation had been portrayed as if the ZEMP Project Coordinator (and, recently, EMU) were reporting to ZEMCC, this had not, and could not, be possible for a number of reasons. Policy issues were actually made by the Ministry of Education, with the input of the donor. ZEMCC only *drafted* them "for the consideration of the appropriate decision-maker". Financial issues were also not handled by ZEMCC but the Ministry of Education and the donor on a bilateral basis. In fact, at the operational level, it was the Finnish Project Coordinator who single-handedly handled the project budget, including updates and revisions. He also coordinated all local disbursements of the project. Project implementation measures were handled bilaterally or trilaterally by the government; the implementing agencies (mainly ZEMP and FINNIDA) and other co-operating donors (e.g., SIDA, NORAD and ODA). The role of ZEMCC was definitely very peripheral.

Against the above background, ZEMCC meetings only discussed in very general way a mixed agenda of issues covering budgeting and policy questions while the really crucial policy issues were handled and decided outside ZEMCC. Indeed, it was evident that ZEMCC was more of a coordinating forum (hence its name) in charge of technical implementation issues than an organ with the mandate (and ability) to handle policy, planning and strategy aspects of ZEMP. In fact, investigations revealed that ZEMCC had not participated actively in ZEMP's annual reviews.

The leaving of decision-making functions of ZEMP to a diverse number of agencies outside the project's immediate implementation circle had tended to weaken its management structure. As a result of the absence of a strong decision-making body in charge of ZEMP activities, it was not surprising that the Project Coordinator had assumed overriding powers over almost all aspects of the project's decision-making and other management functions to a level that he had tended to overshadow those Zambians who were supposedly his superiors.

Lastly, the government organisational framework within which ZEMP operated had compromised and continued to hinder the effectiveness of donor support to educational materials production and procurement. This report has earlier highlighted the peculiar manner in which the full establishment and support of EMU was handled by the government. The subsequent creation of MEPSU did not change much. Although the FINNIDA Education Sector Support Programme (ESSP) Supervisory Board approved the government request in mid-1994 to have ZEMP extended by one year beyond 1994 when it was originally planned to cease, no serious effort was made to strengthen the newly created MEPSU. Thus, as the April–June 1994 Quarterly Report of ZEMP observed, "the establishment and position of MEPSU as the Ministry of Education procurement unit has still not received proper acknowledgement in the Ministry. MEPSU is not included in the organisational chart and its development does not receive appropriate support from the Ministry of Education management."

It is worthy of note that by the end of 1994, the role of MEPSU within the Ministry of Education activities remained quite confused. Firstly, it was evident that ZEMP had met erratically since the creation of MEPSU. Similarly, the newly created MEPSU Technical Committee, when it meets, is usually short of Ministry of Education and donor representation. Thirdly, it seems that the MEPSU Technical Committee's functions duplicate those of ZEMCC, a phenomenon that introduces serious decision-making confusion. Fourthly and, perhaps, more importantly, according to the Ministry of Education restructuring policy position as of the beginning of 1995, the future of MEPSU was no longer certain under the conditions where the Ministry sees itself as being responsible only for policy issues and resource distribution. The Ministry of Education's policy document on the education sector as a whole has been in draft form up to now (January 1996)[48] and it is not yet clear whether the proposal to decentralise procurement procedures in the context of the plan to establish school and district management boards will culminate in the complete elimination of MEPSU.

Local level

One important factor that seems to influence the performance of an externally-assisted project is the degree to which there is effective coordination and dialogue between the headquarters and the lower level organs that are involved in project implementation. The relationship between the donor agency; government line ministries; and the provincial district and project level actors appears to be important in aid effectiveness. In this respect, this study made a rather detailed examination of how ZEMP coordinated its activities with respect to the production and supply of books to schools. Figure 4.1 shows the existing relational interface between the main actors/ levels as of mid-1995.[49]

A number of aspects are noteworthy. Theoretically, the ZEMP books distribution modality is as follows. MEPSU at the Ministry of Education headquarters is in charge of the overall distribution of the programme's books throughout the country. It gives books to ZEPH that, in turn, distributes them through either the District Education Officer or the Zonal Distribution Centres. The latter, in turn, sends them to primary schools. For secondary schools, ZEPH delivers directly to them. In this arrangement, the ZEMP

[48] This is in spite of the fact that it was presented for public discussion by the Ministry of Education in mid-1995.

[49] It is worthy of note that while much of this Chapter is based on ZEMP's structure up to the end of 1993, this Section of the Report is based on data that was collected in August 1995. Nevertheless, apart from MEPSU, the rest of the structures represented in Figure 4.1 existed during the period upon which much of the analysis is based (i.e. up to 1993).

Office serves as an advisory body and participates in the financial management aspects of the production and distribution functions.

In the above process, records are generated regarding which book titles are sent to where and receipts are exchanged for records purposes (see Figure 4.1). These records are periodically sent (usually monthly) to MEPSU in Lusaka either directly or via the District Education Officers.[50]

The actual number of books that are sent to schools by MEPSU is guided, to some degree, by school enrolments as reported by schools themselves. Every year, MEPSU sends a questionnaire to schools on enrolments and book inventories. In this questionnaire, schools provide their enrolment figures and the total number of books received as well as the shortfall in actual demand. At the end of this exercise, MEPSU produces consolidated data on enrolment by province, district and zonal distribution centre.

Generally, the above *modus operandi* has managed to generate considerable useful data for planning purposes. However, operationally, this study has established that there exist a number of organisational and technical problems that have continued to weaken the effectiveness of the ZEMP operational structure as represented in Figure 5.1. Firstly, at the headquarters level, the main complaint of MEPSU concerns inadequate staffing. Out of the eight officers reportedly required to manage the unit effectively, only five are in place. Secondly, there is hardly any coordination between MEPSU's activities and those of other donors in the book supply function. For example, UNICEF that provides supplementary readers to schools does so outside the MEPSU framework. While no serious problems were reported about this situation, indications are that MEPSU would be more comfortable with an arrangement that coordinates and harmonises donor activities in the entire area of school book supply.

Thirdly, still at the headquarters level, it was established that a good number of District Education Officers have failed to either supply MEPSU with the information that is required on the enrolment and book inventory questionnaire or, when this was done, data arrived so late as to make their usability for book distribution purposes redundant. It was reported by the ZEMP Project Coordinator that 25 out of the 61 districts in the country did not submit details about student numbers for 1995 by mid-August that year.[51] Consequently, the MEPSU, at least for 1995, received less than 60% of the data that it uses to guide its book distribution system.

Fourthly, the ability of schools to collect their book allocation from either District Education Officers' offices or the Zone Distribution Centres varies

---

[50] In Kitwe, E.T. Katilungu, Education Officer, Kitwe DEO Office, stated that, for that district, they send the monthly returns regarding books received to the Planning Unit of the Ministry of Education in Lusaka rather than to MEPSU. The justification for this variation in procedures was not made clear.

[51] Interviews with M. Ferns, Project Coordinator, ZEMP, Lusaka, 25 August 1995.

from district to district. For Ndola schools (all of which collect their ZEMP books from the District Education Office not from ZDCs), the Regional Manager reported a 90% collection rate.[52] However, serious concerns almost across the board were reported:

> Sometimes books that we need for the first term arrive in the third term. Therefore, if they send us more of the same title [the following] year, we get more books of one type than we actually need. This happens quite often even after giving them [i.e. MEPSU] the required details on their questionnaire.[53]

Similar sentiments were reported at Chibombo Primary School (Kabwe Rural) which also serves as the area's ZDC:

> This year we have not received any books ... They sometimes supply us with wrong books. We have kept Tonga books for a year now but no one has come to collect them despite reminders.[54]

A different dimension of the same problem was reported by the Deputy Head of Liteta Primary School in Kabwe Rural:

> There is no coordination between the number and type of books that the Ministry [of Education] gives us and the immediate needs of the school. They never even write to us as to when the books we require should be expected. We just wait, often for many months until they suddenly appear.[55]

Two important aspects surface from the above reports. Firstly, there is evidently little communication between MEPSU in Lusaka and the District Education Offices, on the one hand, and schools, on the other, regarding the latter's book requirements beyond the standard annual questionnaire. The problem seems to be two-way. While MEPSU at the headquarters rarely communicates with lower level actors in the book distribution chain due to a host of reasons,[56] the lower level officials are not entirely innocent either as they seem to make little effort to communicate their problems and needs to the headquarters. For example, when the Deputy Head at Chibombo Primary School was asked why she did not enquire from MEPSU why her school did not receive their book allocation for so long, her response was: "we just wait for the vehicle to come," an indication of either complete resignation due to past disappointing experience or the assumption that it is the centre that "knows" what to do prevails.

---

[52] Interview with A. Chabula, Regional Manager, Ndola, 17 August 1995. It is worth observing, however, that the rate of book collection refers to books actually distributed by MEPSU and received by the distribution centres. It says little about whether or not the needed books are distributed and on time.

[53] Interview with H.K. Mutale, District Education Officer, Ndola District, 17 August, 1995.

[54] Interview with A.B. Muwowo, Deputy Head and C. Mukuka, Zone Coordinator, Chibombo Primary School, 18 August 1995. Note that the Tonga books referred to were supplied to a non-Tonga teaching school.

[55] Interview with J.B. Musonda, Deputy Head, Liteta Primary School, 18 August 1995.

[56] These include MEPSU's understaffing; a rather unclear recognition of the Unit in the Ministry of Education's structure, rendering it financial support limited; etc.

Another example of the weak dialogue between the headquarters and the district level was illustrated by the case in Kitwe where the District Education Office confessed to not seeing the relationship between the school enrolment and books inventory questionnaire that they receive from MEPSU, on the one hand, and the actual number of ZEMP books that schools actually receive, on the other. For that office, the data on the questionnaire was conceived of as being purely for general planning purposes. Consequently, their monthly and quarterly reports on books received are sent to the Ministry of Education Planning Unit and not to MEPSU as is expected. Their general argument, shared by several other school authorities interviewed, was that enrolment figures are too indicative and say very little about *actual* book demand by schools. The suggested solution is to actually ask schools what their actual needs are as this would more directly reveal the demand profile. Cases of overenrolment are quite widespread in a good number of schools and the increased book demand caused by this factor is rarely captured by enrolment figures that are reported before the additional pupils are taken on. Besides, schools reported that books that are received by them and which they may still possess from the previous years are rarely taken into account by enrolment-based demand estimation methods. The erratic and unpredictable supply of books to schools (in terms of the uncertainty regarding which titles shall actually be received and when) has forced school authorities to hoard books and release only a "sizeable" quantity to pupils in any given year for fear of the likely possibility of not receiving any the following year. Consequently, per capita book utilisation by pupils is usually low irrespective of whether MEPSU has actually sent enough books for each school child. To the extent that this development compromises the ultimate goal of ZEMP, namely, improving the learning environment in schools by way of book supply, the importance of improving the predictability by school authorities of books availability and supply cannot be overemphasized. Coordination and communication between the different actors in this activity (particularly between MEPSU, DEO, and ZDCs) is critical.

Fifthly, there is a general weak link between Zonal Distribution Centres and schools. This problem is particularly acute in rural areas due to poor access roads and the non-availability of transport. Once books are left at ZDCs, it remains the responsibility of the school to find a way of collecting their allocation. Complicating the problem is the poor telecommunication system that makes ZDCs usually unable to inform schools when their books have arrived.[57]

[57] This problem was reported in Western Province (Interview with M. Mubiana, ZEPH Branch Manager, Mongu, and K.S. Ngonda, Senior Inspector of Schools, Western Province); Central Province (interview with S. Mwangana, ZEPH Branch Manager, Kabwe); and Copperbelt province (interview with J.N. Mumba, ZEPH Manager, Kitwe).

Lastly, a more fundamental problem that affects the objectives of ZEMP has less to do with the actual books delivered than with whether the quality of learning has improved as the result of the programme's books support to schools. This aspect is partially determined by how many books actually reach the pupils/classroom (not necessarily the school). Per capita book utilisation earlier referred to becomes important in the determination of a particular book title's utility value. Two revelations during the course of this study suggested some weaknesses at this level. First, a lot of ZEMP books have found themselves on the illegal/black market, particularly in the Copperbelt and Lusaka Provinces. Both Ndola and Kitwe ZEPH Regional managers reported the "large presence" of their "not for sale" books on the black market.[58] Generally, ZEPH does not see itself as being responsible for checking whether books are reaching the classroom or not. In the opinion of the ZEPH Regional Manager for the Copperbelt:

> ... it is not our responsibility to check if books are reaching the children. It is the responsibility of the Ministry of Education and their Inspectors [of School]. The liaison between us and the Ministry to monitor book disappearance is weak. [At present], there is no accountability at the level of DEOs and schools and, therefore, books can easily disappear.[59]

An interview with a Senior Inspector of Schools suggested that, in most cases, inspectors rarely check whether books reach school and that they are being utilised by the pupils.[60] Whether at the headquarters or school levels, there appears to be no in-built and effective monitoring and evaluation mechanism that is aimed at ensuring that the objectives of ZEMP/MEPSU with regard to the use of their books are realised.

The other noteworthy aspect concerns the role of ZEPH as the ZEMP book distributor. During interviews with ZEPH Regional Managers, there appeared to be a mounting concern regarding the present arrangement. ZEPH's rather contradictory role under the liberalised system (i.e. the free distribution of "not-for-sale" books to schools and, at the same time, selling the very same titles under its own commercial activities)[61] has caused some anxiety among ZEPH officials that feel that the "free" books are killing their own market. Their commercial morale is worsened by the presence of the "free" books on the black market. In other words, ZEPH is given the mandate to distribute for free a product which competes with its own business, a phenomenon that could threaten the Publishing House's commitment to the

58 Interview with A. Chabula, ZEPH Regional Manager, Ndola, and J.N. Mumba, ZEPH Branch Manager, Kitwe.

59 Interview with A. Chabula, op. cit.

60 Interview with K.S. Ngonda, Senior Inspector of Schools, Mongu, 24 August 1995. This was further endorsed by the Deputy Head of Liteta Primary School who reported that inspectors do not ask about how ZEMP books are used.

61 The only difference between the titles is that the ones they sell are not stamped 'not-for-sale'.

discharge of this assignment. Whether the government has recognised this aspect as worth resolving was not apparent.

SUSTAINABILITY OF *ZEMP*

The sustainability of ZEMP beyond donor support is determined partly by the ability of the project to generate the required resources from a variety of sources, particularly those internal to the country. At least up to the end of 1993, the project was organised in such a way that the two principal donors (FINNIDA and SIDA) were dominating its resource base in terms of the supply of financial, technological, and human resources that were needed for the production and distribution of textbooks and exercise books. The main explanation for this was that the government allocations to CDC for materials development had always been insufficient while ZEPH remained riddled with its own poor management structure and performance resulting in the company's failure to operate efficiently and profitably. Educational materials at ZEPH generally took too long to be released also due to the low publishing and printing capacity of the company. Where the government Tender Board had to come in, one of the major problems was that the sub-contracting process employed was so overbureaucratic that it adversely affected the speed of materials production.

Perhaps more restraining was the low level of counterpart funds that were budgeted for educational materials in the government budget. It has been the norm over the years under the ZEMP system for schools to fail to receive sufficient financial resources to meet their book requirements. It is noteworthy that even in cases where books are distributed free of charge, many of them have failed to reach the schools as they stay at the zonal distribution centres due to a variety of reasons ranging from lack of transport to simply poor information flow regarding when the books are ready for collection.

Notwithstanding the above concerns, two positive steps have been accepted by the government towards ensuring the sustainability of ZEMP upon the withdrawal of external support. Firstly, the government is attempting to decentralise the production of educational materials from the state organs to the book industry in Zambia. Theoretically, this would allow the Ministry of Education to perform a more *planning* than operational role.

Secondly, the policy of liberalisation in Zambia has resulted in changes at the book distribution level with new innovations that signal the rejection of centrally-controlled distribution systems. In its 1993 annual review of the Educational Materials sub-programme, for example, SIDA expressly stated that it will pay, through the EMU (under the Ministry of Education) production costs of educational materials while the books distribution costs shall be given to schools through the Provincial Education Officer's offices. Although further refinements to this new concept (fully endorsed by the government) are being looked at, SIDA, being the main donor responsible for meeting the cost of book distribution, is looking for effective ways of enabling schools to attain effective control of their finances. The present proposal is that funds for exercise books shall be disbursed directly to each district according to pupil enrolments. Each District Education Officer shall then buy his/her district's required books and then distribute them. The new system is hoped to encourage suppliers to establish sales outlets at the local level, thus, promoting a more effective and decentralised system of distribution.

Notwithstanding the government's policy of liberalising book publishing and procurement, the experience over the 1992–94 period indicates little practical results. According to the January–March 1994 *Quarterly Report* of ZEMP:

> ... over the 1993–94 period, major delays were witnessed in the government's initiative to adopt publishing- and procurement-related policy especially in terms of the integration of the private publishers. Tendering procedures were also not given much attention by the government. This frustrated ZEMP's efforts to move into the liberalised mode of doing things.[62]

Thirdly, it has further been accepted by both the government and donors that beyond what is contributed by the state in the production and distribution of school books, parents/users must be invited to contribute through cost-sharing. It is noteworthy, however, that SIDA is still committed to supplying free of charge three exercise books per child per year at the primary school level. Interviews with ZEPH Regional Managers and District Education Officers during mid-1995 revealed there is an increasing appreciation of the need to charge the pupils even a token amount for the "free" books to improve on the needed sense of responsibility vis-à-vis the use of these books.

Lastly, ZEMP's mode of support to educational materials development has radically changed following the liberalisation of the educational publishing industry in Zambia. Most importantly, ZEPH and CDC are now being perceived as only two of the many educational materials providers. In this regard, FINNIDA and SIDA support to the development of educational materials is no longer restricted to these two government-run/owned organisations. These donors have made it explicitly clear that, through the MEPSU at the Ministry of Education, donor funds shall supply paper and other raw materials to ZEPH or other manufacturers for the production of educational materials. In a similar vein, donor funds shall be used to acquire services of suppliers of educational materials from the region and overseas if and when locally-based suppliers are not able to provide adequate service (in terms of quality and quantity).

---

62 ZEMP, *Quarterly Report,* January–March 1994.

THE AID RELATIONSHIP IN THE *ZEMP*

The design of ZEMP was such that to a very high degree it depended on a tight integration with various government bodies in the educational system of Zambia. Starting from the level of the Ministry of Education down to the District Educational Officer. The history of ZEMP, as it unfolded, revealed an aid relationship which was quite far from this ideal state of affairs. The project was characterised by lack of involvement by all concerned organisational levels in the Zambian administration. It was particularly revealing to find that the aid relationship never really ventured down to include the intended beneficiaries of the project activities. At the same time no one really bothered to rectify the situation. The donors, FINNIDA and SIDA, seemed content to have ZEMP established as an enclave within the educational system. The Zambian government, as it turned out, adopted a policy of "not rocking the boat". It probably had good reasons for doing so, in spite of the fact that it at times had strong opinions about what was happening. Voicing its concerns could have meant that it also opened up for criticism regarding the way it fulfilled its obligations in the project. The ZEMP story shows how the government failed to deliver in terms of an efficient administration. Not because it had become uninterested in the project, but because it could not mobilise the needed local resources. For good reasons then, the government played it safe and preferred a conflict mode characterised by withdrawal and/or suppression. The outcome was an aid relationship where the key parties never really ventured into a serious and constructive dialogue with each other. The result was a project with limited possibilities for sustainability.

Chapter 6

The Western Province Water Supply and Sanitation Programme

INTRODUCTION

The Zambian government is giving a high priority to the supply of clean water to both urban and rural communities. The Norwegian Agency for Development Cooperation (NORAD) support to the Western Province Water Supply programme constitutes the main focus of this case study. In May 1975, the Zambia government made a request to the Norwegian government for support towards the improvement of water supply to Western Province, a remote rural region covering 126,386 square kilometres and representing 17% of the country's total land mass. Approximately 75% of Western Province's population are rural.

In September 1975, a pre-feasibility study was undertaken by a three-man NORAD team that visited the province for five days. It was this study that recommended a limited NORAD programme of support for the rehabilitation of seven township water supply schemes and the construction of 700 well points in the rural parts of the province. With very limited data available (even among NORAD officials in Lusaka) regarding the process of initiating Norwegian support to the water sector in Western Province, it appears that it was the initial pre-feasibility study's findings that constituted the basis for the first bilateral agreement between Zambia and Norway that was signed in July 1977. The first phase of the programme, running over the 1977–79 period, began immediately upon the signing of the Agreement. The programme has passed through five phases and is currently in the phasing out stage. Table 6.1 shows the phases and the amount of Norwegian Kroner allocated. As can be seen from the table, a three-year phasing out period, covering 1994–96, is currently in operation.

PROGRAMME OBJECTIVES

In broad terms, the NORAD support to Western Province has two main components, namely, the *Rural Water Supply* and the *Township Water Supply*. These components are briefly described below. After this, a deeper analysis of the programme concentrates mainly on the rural component of NORAD support.

Table 6.1. *Norwegian support to Western Province Water Supply and Sanitation Programme, 1977–1994* (NOK million)

Phase	Period	Allocation
I	1977–79	17.2
II	1980–83	85.0
III	1984–85	45.0
IV	1986–89	100.0
V	1990–93	37.0
Phasing Out	1994–96	11.0*

* proposed
Source: DWA/NORAD, *Water Supply and Sanitation Programme: Western Province. Proposed NORAD support in the period 1994–96.* Mongu: Provincial Water Engineer/RB Consultants Int. A/S, February 1994.

Rural water supply

This component of the NORAD-supported Water Supply and Sanitation programme began in 1977 covering three main elements, namely, rural well-points; micro projects; and secondary settlements. The overall objective of the rural well-points sub-component is to enable rural communities in Western Province access reliable and clean water supply. Complementary to this broad objective is the target of achieving sustainability in the operation and maintenance of water supply by the rural community themselves. Related to this goal is the objective of achieving improved hygiene practices related to water and sanitation.

The micro projects sub-component aims to assist those rural communities, accounting for about 25% of Western Province's population, that are not eligible under the handpump programme to develop improved traditional sources of water. The sub-component essentially involves the construction of collars and cover slabs for traditional hand-dug wells. Lastly, with respect to the secondary settlements sub-component to the main objective entails the provision of reliable and safe water supply to four secondary rural centres in Western Province with population concentrations of around 3,000 people. It involves the supply of communal stand-pipes.

Township water supply

This component of the Water Supply and Sanitation Programme has four elements, namely, (a) the supply of water to six district townships; (b) Mongu and Limulunga townships (i.e. the two townships in Western Province with the largest population concentration, accounting for 27% of the province's population); (c) Sanitation I; and (d) Sanitation II. With regard to the Township supplies sub-component, the programme's main objective is to rehabilitate their water supply systems so as to increase their distribution networks' capacity. A complementary objective of this sub-component is the enhancement of the operation and maintenance capacity of the existing indigenous authorities in order to make them self-sustaining. Full cost-recovery of operational expenses is the target goal at this level.

The main objective of the Sanitation I component is to employ community participatory approaches to attain improved sanitary conditions around communally-owned stand-pipes in townships. Sanitation II, in turn, aims at improving sanitary conditions by popularising the use of improved pit latrines.

PROGRAMME DESIGN AND PERFORMANCE: 1977–84

Mobilisation stage

The current operations of the NORAD supported Western Province Water Supply and Sanitation Programme ought to be comprehended within the context of the two main distinct stages it has gone through and the degree to which positive responses to critical evaluations have improved considerably the prospects for programme effectiveness and sustainability.

In December 1977, the Norwegian consulting firm, Ostlandskonsult A/S (later called Interconsult A/S) was hired by NORAD to plan and design the water supply programme for the province. Seven expatriate personnel were also recruited by NORAD in 1977. They consisted of one Programme Coordinator; one Workshop Superintendent; two Senior Mechanics; one Drilling Superintendent; one Building Superintendent; and one Teaching Instructor. While the Project Coordinator was stationed some 600 kilometres away in the capital city of Zambia, the seven team members were posted to Mongu, the provincial headquarters of Western Province.

The initiation of Phase I of the project (1977–79) was delayed by factors that included:

- — difficulties in finding qualified Norwegian personnel for recruitment;
- — problems of Norwegian personnel adapting to local conditions;
- — slowness in the acquisition and delivery of drill rigs;
- — absence of an operational plan for the implementation of the rural water supply programme;
- — virtual absence of back-up support to expatriate personnel from Norway.[63]

Below is a descriptive analysis of a number of attributes of the programme's operations prior to 1985.

---

63 Fergus, M. et al., 1987.

Programme design

Perhaps the most important noteworthy weakness of the programme during the 1977–84 period was the absence of a comprehensive project document that should have provided the required guidance to the programme. The feasibility study that was undertaken in 1975 was basically technical and never took into account such other relevant aspects for project effectiveness as the organisational, economic, social and cultural considerations. Similarly, the programme's feasibility study was undertaken by the donor's representatives with no reported participation of the recipient (both central and provincial governments and target communities at the local level). It was also hastily carried out (following a few days' visit to Western Province) and clearly demonstrated the absence of the traditionally needed details to establish meaningfully the scope of the activities that the project administrators ambitiously embarked upon. Even more contradictory, in spite of their limited utility, the actual "feasibility" studies were actually undertaken *after* the bilateral agreement was signed and the major programme premises and assumptions already conceptualised. It was typically the case in which the *solutions* were established before the *problem* was clearly determined.

Programme management

Serious weaknesses in project management during the pre-1985 period were observable. Firstly, the programme, although supposedly located under the Department of Water Affairs (DWA) headquarters, was operated centrally from Lusaka by the Norwegian Project Coordinator. It was, thus, operating quite independently of the government's Provincial Water Engineer. It is noteworthy in this respect that when NORAD arrived in Western Province, DWA was already involved in water supply in the region. Thus, the donor agency introduced a parallel system since there was no coordination between the two providers of this service. Interviews in Western Province established that the parallel structure introduced by NORAD was highly resented by locally-based government officials in DWA.[64] The 1987 evaluation report of the programme also noted this state of affairs:

> The Western Province Water Supply programme has, to a large extent, been autonomous of the Government control at national level, district level and community level. In the past, the programme has operated outside the administrative, financial and technical structure of Government ... There is evidence to show that there has been a strong tendency in the programme to try to circumvent the existing system for the sake of productivity and efficiency. This has been done at the expense of long-term targets like institution-building and integration which are necessary in order to sustain development in the future. Similarly, it means the programme in its initial years has built

[64] Interview with Mr M.S. Muyendekwa, Provincial Water Engineer, Mongu, June 1994.

> up a 'dependence syndrome' which is difficult to dismantle quickly without causing major problems of disruption.[65]

Against the above background, the programme's organisation and activities during the 1977–85 period could be characterised as an absence of:

— an operational plan
— clearly specified project targets and indicators of achievement
— monitoring mechanisms such as pre-planned evaluations
— community participation in project activities
— absence of project management continuity.

In essence, the Rural Water Supply component of the programme during this initial period was founded on an engineering approach whereby water supply was perceived as being essentially a technical problem and not a social commodity. Consequently, the role of the beneficiaries in direct provision was not seen as an important component of the delivery system. This resulted in the marginalisation of the community in the programme's planning, implementation, maintenance, monitoring, and evaluation. The beneficiaries at the local level were not involved in both the selection of the technology used and the actual location of the water supply sources. On the basis of very crude estimates and without generating and/or utilising socio-economic baseline data, the foreign 'experts' proceeded in determining the community's water demand and then concentrated on the construction of boreholes and wells.

Without community involvement as well as inappropriate technology choices (a diversity of handpump models were acquired resulting in costly maintenance) and given the poor record of maintenance of equipment, the programme realised limited positive results in spite of constructing more than 200 boreholes and 220 shallow wells and having spent over NOK 50 million by 1985. In fact, mainly because of poor communication with the community, the programme was initially greeted with a certain degree of resistance from none other than the targeted beneficiaries themselves.

In the light of the above poor record of performance, NORAD initiated an evaluation of the programme in 1984 and radical recommendations towards improving the programme's effectiveness resulted from the analysis. The recommendations included the following:

— a new implementation plan with clear targets for manpower development; water supply coverage; and maintenance activities should be drawn;

— the programme should gradually be integrated into the government structure by making it part of the Provincial Water Engineer's organisational structure in Western Province;

[65] Fergus, M. et al., 1987, op. cit.

— community involvement principles should be adopted in the programme's rural component which should include health, education and sanitation aspects;

— there was need to emphasise operation and maintenance (O & M) in the programme's activities;

— development of an elaborate training programme that is related to the official Zambian system. On-the-job training for local personnel should be an integral part of the supervisor's responsibility;

— the Lusaka-based Norwegian company that implemented the programme (Ostlandskonsult) should be moved to the provincial headquarters of Western Province (Mongu);

— a monitoring and evaluation system should be designed that would be used to establish the technical and social achievements and weaknesses of the programme; and

— the need to develop a viable and realistic programme strategy that would consider, *inter alia*, water supply cost efficiency; balancing the programme's implementation capacity; establishing advisory committees at both the provincial and district levels; enhancing inter-sectoral cooperation and collaboration; motivating local communities; and promoting women's involvement at all levels of the programme, especially in decision-making.

POSITIVE RE-ORIENTATION: POST 1985 PERIOD

The criticism levelled against the NORAD-supported Western Province Water Supply and Sanitation Programme during its pre-1985 period was appreciated by both the Zambian government and NORAD and this resulted in a completely new orientation of both the organisational structure and operational approach of the programme. The post-1985 revised programme also overhauled the programme objectives. The key changes included the following:

— the introduction of the Community Education and Participation (CEP) component as an important element towards the achievement of sustainable programme operation and maintenance, in addition to the promotion of improved hygiene practices at the local community level;

— integration of the programme into the government system;

— identification of indicators of project achievement; and

— establishment of strong linkages across different sectors in the province.

A closer look at the above four areas would underline not only the programme's post-1985 unique ability to accommodate recipient-led concerns about its earlier weaknesses but also the programme's current strengths in terms of effectiveness and potential sustainability beyond donor support.

COMMUNITY EDUCATION AND PARTICIPATION (*CEP*)

Perhaps the most novel step taken towards programme effectiveness and sustainability from the recipient's stand point was the establishment in April 1985 of the Community Education and Participation (CEP) component in the programme. CEP is founded on the premises that the water consumer is the most important and should, therefore, be the most active (or activated) participant in all the various steps of the process of improved water supply and access. Organisationally, CEP operates through the concept of 'teams' that are physically located at the Zambian government's DWA and accountable to the DWA Programme Coordinator. The CEP teams consist of officials that possess a diversity of skills and are mainly on secondment from other ministries. They include nurses and health assistants from the Ministry of Health; extension workers from the Ministry of Agriculture; and teachers from the Ministry of Education. Bricklayers and plumbers have also been recruited and trained by the programme to complement the efforts of the CEP teams.

Operationally, the CEP teams' more social functions are interwoven with the engineering component of the programme in such a way that the required social, economic, and cultural considerations are taken into account. For example, CEP teams usually precede the drilling teams in order to 'prepare' the community adequately for the new development in their area. Once the project has been carried out (e.g. the installation of a borehole and pump), the CEP team also provide the backstopping function of follow-ups focusing on, *inter alia*, hygiene education and facility maintenance by the beneficiaries themselves. Each village covered has a Village Maintenance Team (VMT) that is responsible for pump maintenance, in addition to providing local building materials. A comprehensive training programme for VMTs is being facilitated by the Water Supply and Sanitation Programme in order to strengthen the target communities' capacity to manage their water facilities. In general, therefore, the main activities of CEP are as follows:

- facilitating health education on water and sanitation (also in schools);
- facilitating the community's participation in planning, implementation and maintenance of programme activities;
- facilitating community organisation through meetings, seminars and workshops;
- assisting communities on how to generate incomes needed for maintaining their handpumps;

— training of other extension workers that are required in the community motivation activities;
— enhancing inter-sectoral cooperation in water supply and health and sanitation issues; and
— designing monitoring and evaluation systems in order to easily determine programme impact.

Under the present arrangement, each ministry is responsible for the remuneration of the individual that it has seconded to the Provincial CEP team since DWA has no positions in its establishment for the recruitment of permanent CEP team members. At the district level, there also exist CEP teams (i.e. district CEP teams). However, the teams at this level are not recognised within the governmental establishment and are, therefore, financed by the programme.

Against the above background, although there are factors that are still threatening the programme's sustainability (see below), the introduction of the CEP concept in the NORAD-financed programme has evidently enhanced the opportunities of its effectiveness. Indeed, given the pre-1985 programme experience, the introduction of the 'software' component through CEP has demonstrated that there are few chances of project effectiveness and sustainability in this type of programme if it is exclusively based on technical inputs.

INTEGRATION INTO THE GOVERNMENT SYSTEM

The degree to which the Western Province Water Supply and Sanitation programme was integrated into the government system would ultimately determine its prospects for being sustainable. Since 1985, serious efforts have been made to ensure that the programme becomes an integral part DWA. However, the initial NORAD uneasiness regarding operating under the government system did not go away easily. For example, before the operations could be integrated into the Provincial Water Engineer's supervision, NORAD recommended to the Zambian government (and it was unsuspectingly accepted) to have the existing person (i.e. the Provincial Water Engineer) replaced by a Norwegian. This was effected and the new expatriate Norwegian occupied this strategic government position over the 1985–87 period. The NORAD-supported programme operated under him. Interviews in Western Province during the course of this study revealed that this arrangement introduced a certain level of resentment among provincial government officials.

The post of Programme Coordinator has since been localised following the appointment of an indigenous hydrogeologist at the provincial level. He is presently the official who is in charge of project management and the supervision of drilling activities and provincial and district CEP teams.

Similarly, the position of the Rural Water Supply Coordinator has been localised and he operates within the government system and reports to the Provincial Water Engineer. At the district level, the rural programme is administered by the government official in charge of water affairs at this level.

PROGRAMME ACHIEVEMENT INDICATOR

Following the poor performance and monitoring record of the 1977–85 period, the Water Supply and Sanitation Programme has introduced rudimentary systems of project monitoring and reporting. For example, in November 1988, a group exercise reworked the programme's development and immediate objectives as well as designing indicators for project achievement. A logical framework matrix of the rural water supply development in the province under the programme was worked out.

Notwithstanding the above initiative, one still observes from the programme documents that the programme's objectives are still being stated in such broad terms as to make monitoring and employment of achievement indicators difficult. Similarly, the programme's progress reporting has tended to be unsystematic and usually hardly refers to set targets. Indeed, as the April 1994 Fourth Annual Meeting for the programme reported, "NORAD made a general comment that it would like the Progress Reports to be more streamlined to make it easier to get the comparison between work plan, budget, targets and achievements".[66]

The sentiments of the 1992 programme evaluation team on a related subject of improved sanitation sheds more light on this concern:

> The fact that there are no physical indicators to measure access to improved sanitation demonstrates the Programme's lack of concern for sanitation matters ... In 15 years, not a single initiative besides the educational work of the CEP team members has been taken to investigate ways to improve excreta disposal. This has undermined the overall impact of the rural programme.[67]

What the above concerns suggest is that the programme's procedures still required improvement.

INTER-SECTORAL LINKAGES

Following the programme's pre-1985 experience, a more effective rural water supply delivery system that takes into account the pivotal role of various stakeholders was put in place. As the 1992 programme evaluation team observed:

> ... of particular note are the linkages which have been established horizontally between different government departments and the professional cadres

66 GRZ/NORAD, 1994, p. 3.

67 Kruger, A. et al., 1992.

> at provincial and district level, and of linkages established vertically between provinces, district and the community in support of the overall objectives of the programme.[68]

Perhaps at the centre of this inter-sectoral collaboration success is the decision by both the government and NORAD to establish WASHE committees at both the provincial and district levels, thus allowing for a good stakeholder representation in project planning, implementation and monitoring. These committees draw their membership from such government wings as the Ministry of Health; Ministry of Community Development and Social Services; Ministry of Agriculture and Water Development, etc. Chaired by senior government officials, these committees have given legitimacy to inter-sectoral cooperation that is needed particularly at the programme implementation level. The functions of CEP teams further consolidate inter-sectoral participation in the activities of the NORAD-supported programme. This type of collaboration also strengthens the community's perception of the programmes as *theirs* rather than a 'NORAD' project (as it was initially perceived), a phenomenon that enhances its sustainability beyond donor support.

PROGRAMME SUSTAINABILITY AND EFFECTIVENESS

Performance criteria

One of the most important criteria of project effectiveness, particularly from the point of view of the recipient country, is the degree to which it is sustainable. Sustainability in this regard entails the programme's ability to deliver an appropriate level of benefits using the most cost-effective but socially acceptable means for an extended period of time after major financial, managerial and/or technical assistance from the external donor has been terminated or significantly reduced. Phase V of the NORAD support to the programme ended in 1993 and effective from January 1994, a three-year phasing out period (1994–96) of Norwegian support has been decided upon and is currently in effect. According to NORAD, "the overall objective of the phasing-out period is to achieve sustainability of the present water and sanitation programme in Western Province or to establish an appropriate activity level which continues without donor support".[69]

It is worth noting that according to the phasing out scheme, certain components of the programme may continue to receive support after this period. These include sanitation, the Provincial CEP and the improvement of traditional sources of water supply. Moreover, the head of the NORAD delegation at the April 1994 Annual Meeting of the programme stated that:

---

68 Kruger, A. et al., 1992, op. cit.

69 DWA/NORAD, 1994.

> "NORAD is ... embarking on a National Water Sector programme aiming at providing Norwegian support to the sector in line with national priorities. Western Province," he stressed, "may therefore also in the future get support from NORAD if this is within the national priorities."[70]

In determining the sustainability of the Western Province Water Supply and Sanitation programme, a number of factors and considerations are important. Among the most important ones are:

- the general programme performance up to the time when donor support is withdrawn;
- organisational and institutional capacity considerations particularly with regard to the government's policies and commitment towards the programme. This largely entails the extent to which central, provincial and district level authorities would provide the necessary organisational, institutional and legal framework within which the programme can sustain a reasonable level of service to its target population;
- financial and technological sustainability in terms of the availability of alternative and adequate sources of financing and technological resources upon the withdrawal of NORAD resources and beyond; and
- availability of indigenous human resources to take up the tasks of programme implementation and monitoring.

These four areas are analysed separately below.

General project performance

Initially, the NORAD-supported Western Province Water Supply and Sanitation Programme adopted a largely engineering approach to the delivery of water supply to the target communities. These communities were hardly involved in the programme's planning, implementation, maintenance and monitoring. Nor did the programme possess a clear Operational Plan and achievement indicators to guide implementation. The programme's effectiveness during this initial period (1977–85) was very marginal at both the technical soundness and socio-economic levels.

The post-1985 programme performance saw major positive developments. At the technical level, programme targets have largely been realised. By the end of 1993, about 1,080 functioning wells had been constructed under the programme. These wells serve some 215,000 beneficiaries, which is approximately half of the province's rural population. Additionally, by the end of 1993, eight townships in the province had been supported with new or extended water supplies. Four secondary centres have also been supplied with water by the programme, in addition to which the health and

[70] GRZ/NORAD, 1994, op. cit.

sanitation component has been implemented as it particularly relates to the improvement of the traditional water sources. Perhaps the major weakness at this level has been the earlier reported inability of the programme to design appropriate indicators to gauge the effectiveness of its sanitation component. Generally, however, the programmes' ability to meet its physical targets has been considerable.

Organisational and institutional capacity

Perhaps the strongest attribute of the NORAD-supported programme during the post-1985 period has been the development of elaborate and functioning inter-sectoral linkages that have pooled physical and human resources together through a network of horizontal and vertical links across a broad spectrum of government ministries, districts and stakeholders, including the beneficiaries themselves. The programme's novelty at this level is the degree to which it has taken advantage of community participation through the WASHE committee system and its CEP teams. It is equally noteworthy that over 50% of the CEP teams consist of women. Similarly, at least 50% of the membership of the Village Water Committees are women, thus providing them with an opportunity to participate in planning and decision-making aspects of their felt needs. Within the CEP teams, women are also being trained for, and employed in, such technical jobs as plumbing, metal work and bricklaying. In this regard, the programme is breaking the stereotype of segregated gender roles. Another positive aspect of the programme's organisation is that a clearly defined mechanism of selecting participation in the programme (i.e. which community should be targeted) has been developed and takes due consideration of social, geographical, logistical and technical considerations.

Yet another positive development in relation to the programme's sustainability is the fact that it currently operates under DWA and has, therefore, been fully integrated into the government system. Similarly, all senior programme positions have been localised. Notwithstanding these positive developments, a number of in-built institutional weaknesses seem to threaten the programme's complete sustainability upon the withdrawal of NORAD support. Firstly, the rural water supply sub-programme at the district level is currently being administered by the government official in charge of water affairs in general (i.e. both township and rural water supplies). Consequently, the rural water sub-programme at the district level has no designated coordinator and has to compete for attention with its township counterpart in an environment where the latter almost always receives priority. In fact, it is only the district CEP teams that are dedicated to the rural sub-programme at the district level. And yet—and this is the paradox—this is the very team that is presently not recognised within the establishment of government (see above) despite its holding the key to the success of future sustainability of the water supply delivery system at this level. As of now, the district CEP team are employed by the programme. Should the government fail to absorb these important people into its establishment by the time NORAD funds are withdrawn, one expects a serious disruption of the rural component.

A similar problem, though to a lesser extent, obtains at the provincial level. Most provincial CEP team members are occupying non-establishment positions at DWA and are on secondment from their respective ministries. What this means is that, for the rural water supply and sanitation component, the only full-time person at both the provincial and district levels occupying a line position at DWA is the Programme Coordinator. The current organisational structure of the programme is such that the Rural Water Supply Coordinator (who is a hydrologist) is accountable to the Provincial Water Engineer. What is of concern with respect to the rural water sub-programme's integration into the government system is the fact that it does not have counterpart staff at the DWA headquarters. Consequently, what exists in Western Province with regard to the rural water supply component is a project-oriented structure that functions with considerable autonomy from DWA's overall structure. Under such conditions, a genuine concern could be raised regarding the long-term sustainability of this component of the NORAD-supported programme. As the 1992 programme evaluation team observed,

> ... this raises several questions concerning the long-term sustainability of the rural water supply programme as regards policy formulation, planning and budgeting, establishment of standards, monitoring and evaluation ...[71]

Against the above realisation, although the rural water supply component of the programme has developed an elaborate and effective delivery system, its survival appears to be intimately linked to the continuance of external support since it is yet to be fully integrated into the DWA establishment structure. Its continued dependence on seconded personnel from other ministries also makes it vulnerable as these officials feel insecure about their position in their parent ministries amidst the ongoing restructuring and retrenchment in the civil service in general.

Figure 6.1 outlines the basic features of the working relationships in the project. The existing structure linking the various stakeholders from the headquarters in Lusaka down to the project level in the Western Province water supply programme suggests that there is a further problem of little coordination and harmonisation among them. As of August 1995,[72] the following structure existed. Firstly, at the *national* level in Lusaka, there is the Department of Water Affairs that is headed by a director. Under the

[71] Kruger, A. et al., 1992, op. cit.

[72] This information was collected in August 1995 as a follow up to the earlier fieldwork by the authors.

Director of the Department of Water Affairs at the provincial level is the Provincial Water Engineer. At the provincial level, there are a number of government structures that are expected to play a role in water supply, either directly or indirectly. At the more general level, there is the Provincial Planning Unit (PPU) that falls under the office of the Provincial Permanent Secretary. PPU is supposed to provide the needed provincial planning capacity for all the development programmes in the province. The unit helps in the preparation of project proposals from the districts and is expected to monitor project progress in the entire province.

Figure 6.1. *Actors and relationships in the NORAD supported water programme*

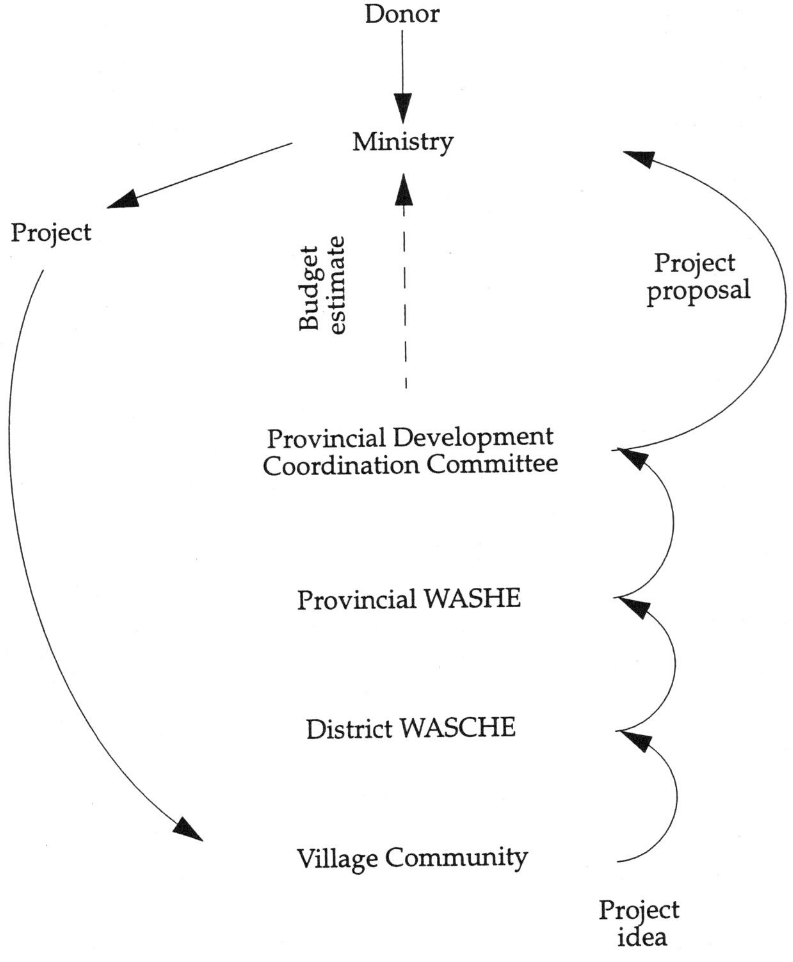

Specifically with respect to the water sector, the Provincial Water Engineer is answerable to both the Provincial Permanent Secretary and the Director of the Department of Water Affairs in Lusaka. Both the Permanent Secretary and the Director receive Quarterly Reports and Annual Reports from the Provincial Water Engineer. Water-related financial resources are channelled to the Provincial Water Engineer from both the Provincial Permanent Secretary and the Director in Lusaka.

At the implementation level, the water programme in the province is integrated into the government system through the Water, Sanitation and Health Education (WASHE) Steering Committee that is under the chairmanship of the Provincial Permanent Secretary. The programme activities are executed by the Provincial Water Engineer. Each district in the Province has its District WASHE Committee and at the village level, the Village Water Committees form part of the WASHE structure. When money is received by the Provincial Water Engineer, expenditure decisions are made by the Provincial WASHE that is chaired by the Provincial Permanent Secretary. The membership of the Provincial WASHE is drawn from the provincial heads of the strategic ministries in the region such as the Ministry of Education; the Ministry of Agriculture; the Department of Water Affairs; etc. Donor organisations that operate at the provincial level are not represented in this Committee although there is an annual meeting with donors. Neither are NGOs represented on these WASHE committees from the province down to the Village Water Committee level. An equally noteworthy aspect is that the Director of the Department of Water Affairs at the headquarters in Lusaka does not receive the reports of the Annual Provincial WASHE Committee meetings. The director, however, attends the annual meetings of the Provincial Water Engineering Department. It is also important to note that since 1990, new financial procedures have been in operation whereby NORAD budget allocations for the programme are disbursed directly to the Provincial Permanent Secretary. Similarly, funds for capital projects are being controlled by DWA and not by NORAD.

To what extent is the above structure coordinated and how much consultation exists at between the headquarters and the project/community level? This study revealed a number of coordination weaknesses that threaten the future sustainability of the water development programme in Western Province. Figure 6.1 shows the relational pattern that existed as of August 1996.

Firstly, donor resources are channelled through the Provincial Water Engineer to the province with little or no involvement of the Department of Water Affairs in Lusaka. Although donor-supported project proposals are negotiated at the centre between the department and the donor agency, actual resource flows are more direct. To this extent, some form of positive decentralisation has been attained. Perhaps the main weakness is connected with the absence of a centralised organ that ensures that activities of various donors in the same sector are monitored and coordinated in such a way that unnecessary duplication is avoided. Secondly, while there appears to be some form of dialogue between the community upwards through the District WASHE to the Provincial WASHE and ultimately to the Department of Water Affairs in Lusaka, there is evidently an absence of actual involvement by the community in the discussion with the donors at the project proposal stage.[73] The concerns of the Provincial Planning Unit Supervisor are quite revealing in this respect:

> There is very little coordination with the centre ... There is a weak link between the centre and the province. The donors and their activities are approved at the national level ... then implementation is done at the province or district level. When it comes to winding-up [the project], the centre is approached but since they were not fully involved [at the implementation stage], they are usually not readily receptive to the requirements of the lower level.[74]

The above concerns were perhaps put more forcefully by the Secretary to the Cabinet in his circular letter announcing the cabinet decision to create Development Coordination Committees at the national; provincial; and district levels:

> It has been observed that over the past years, development programmes at district and provincial levels have been initiated and implemented without adequate consultation and coordination among the various key organisations operating at these levels. Social and economic development activities at district and provincial levels have hitherto suffered from lack of (a) effective coordination between sector ministry/department, local authorities, donors, NGOs, and other agents of development; (b) effective monitoring and reporting systems on the overall developmental effort at district and provincial level; and (c) mechanisms for insuring government responsiveness to local needs in service delivery.[75]

Financial and technological sustainability

The most important strength of the Western Province Water Supply programme is its being designed in such a way that the community is made to appreciate the importance of their contributing, financially and materially, to its success. Firstly, beyond the installation of a borehole and handpump, the beneficiaries perform basic maintenance tasks, in addition to contributing their labour (and materials) to the programme. The role of CEP in this regard is of strategic significance. For example, CEP activities include the task of informing and assisting the community on how to design and operate ventures that could generate the income needed for operating and maintaining their water pumps. In addition, some income is at present

---

73 In the interview with the Provincial Water Engineer, Muyendekwa, in Mongu on 23 August 1995, it was reported that his office rarely meets with PPU for the purpose of coordination. His view is that the latter operates in isolation in most cases. The activities of several other donors, like those of the Dutch and NGOs at the provincial level in the water sector were also reportedly not coordinated with those handled by the office of the Provincial Water Engineer.

74 Interview with Sichone, PPU Supervisor, Mongu, 23 August, 1995.

75 Adamson, A., 1995.

being generated through call-out fees and payments for spares and consumables by the villages. To reduce the cost of community-based maintenance of handpumps, appropriate solutions have been developed particularly towards the standardisation of handpump technology.

Notwithstanding the above positive developments, it is noteworthy that rural communities are generally ill-equipped to shoulder the total costs of their improved water supply systems covering the resources needed for equipment acquisition, drilling operations, and management and maintenance costs. A series of logistical supports covering both operation and maintenance is usually required. In particular, the availability of well-serviced, maintained and adequate transport facilities is important for programme effectiveness and sustainability. In this respect, for the rural water supply where full cost recovery cannot be expected in the near future (unlike in the case of the township component), the government should have both the willingness and ability to take over the task of replenishing such items as programme vehicles that are required by the drilling and CEP teams. The sentiments of the 1994 document that presents the proposed NORAD support during the 1994–96 phasing out period underline this concern:

> The financial sustainability of rural water supply in Western Province is not possible in the near future unless the government participates with financial support as well as with the provision of an operational framework which enables local financing of rural water supply through cost recovery and income generating activities.[76]

The rural community's inability to meet its water supply costs was echoed during interviews with the current Programme Coordinator in charge of the rural component

> ... the main worry here is the [sustainability of] the rural water supply ... We are trying to transfer the costs to the rural communities but the current economic conditions at the household level are compromising their initiatives ... We are worried that we would not be able to acquire spares for rural handpumps if we are to depend exclusively on payments from villagers.[77]

Indigenous human resources

The programme's considerable dependence on community participatory mechanisms in service delivery has been commendable as it used the most abundant resource available in the rural setting, namely, the human resource. Equally significant is the programme's achievement in localising all posts. This would make the complete withdrawal of funding less disruptive of the ongoing activities. More importantly, the programme has maintained

---

76 DWA/NORAD, 1994, op. cit., p. 47.

77 Interview with Mr M K Samani, Hydrologist and Rural Water Supply Coordinator, Mongu, 3 June 1994.

an elaborate artisans training scheme for a diversity of skills including plumbers, mechanics, bricklayers and drillers. Presently, around 100 posts are held by such people. However, these skilled people upon whom the sustainability of the programme partially depends have not been absorbed by the government establishment and their salaries and other remuneration continue to be drawn from the programme's resources. What this means is that if the government fails to absorb these artisans at the end of donor support for the programme, the sustainability of the rural water supply component may be seriously threatened.

It is at the level of more qualified technical personnel that the programme could be faulted. As the 1987 programme evaluation team observed:

> ... because of the short planning horizon and the continual concern for technical performance, not enough attention has been paid to the training of engineers and professionals who can take over the system. The training component has rather been geared towards the production of technicians who can operate the system and maintain the transport function.[78]

In this regard, the programme could have benefited more from increased training of indigenous personnel in more professional fields.

THE AID RELATIONSHIP IN THE WATER AND SANITATION PROGRAMME

In terms of a good aid relationship, this project was off to a bad start. It was a donor-driven initiative, where the appraisal and project formulation stage involved the government only to a limited degree. Even more limited, not to say totally absent, was the involvement of the direct beneficiaries of improved water and sanitation—the people in the villages. During the first seven years the programme reflected an engineering approach to development. The programme was all about establishing water points. Any broader societal concerns were virtually absent from the programme and its activities. Organisationally, the programme resembled the ZEMP. It was mainly managed outside the existing government structures and largely un-coordinated with other similar activities undertaken by the government. Not surprisingly there was a lot of resentment, particularly at the provincial and district levels, created in the process. The aid relationship, such as it was, can only be described as the local parties withdrawing from, or suppressing, conflicts. There were several reasons for this. One had to do with the actual needs in Western Province. Any initiative was welcome which tried to address the basic needs of the people in the province. Naturally the authorities would not take the risk of antagonising the donor and perhaps jeopardise the continuation of the programme. Another reason explaining the conflict pattern, at least as far as the district and provincial levels are

[78] Fergus, M. et al., 1987, op. cit.

concerned, had to do with the fact that the donor and the line ministry seemed to be in agreement with each other.

What seems to have triggered a change in this pattern seems to have been a growing concern within NORAD that things were not going well. A major evaluation seemed to have a catalysing effect in this regard. Steps were then taken, at the initiative of the donor, to radically restructure the programme. Its mode of operation was refocused to the community level, and most of its functions localised. These changes created a new aid relationship, where the target group suddenly found themselves deeply involved in the affairs of the programme. Did these changes suggest better prospects for sustainability? The answer is not entirely positive. The programme is still not fully integrated under the responsible government department. Furthermore, there is the ever present issue of the local resources needed, at the village level for maintaining the water points and at the government level for providing equipment and manpower.

Chapter 7

Drought Emergency in Southern Africa

BACKGROUND

The 1992 drought in Zambia was the worst in living memory and approximately one third of the Zambian population was affected. Lusaka, Southern and Central Provinces were worst hit while the northern part of the country was marginally affected. The result of the drought on food output, particularly on the country's staple grain (maize) was translated into considerably reduced levels of national food supply. As compared to the 1990/91 agricultural season, crop production during 1992 declined by 93% in Southern; 85% in Lusaka; and 80% in Western Provinces. It declined by 79% and 57% in Eastern and Central Provinces, respectively. By June 1992, the Central Statistical Office's survey established that 82% of the households had run out of food in Luangwa and Kalomo districts of Eastern and Southern Provinces, respectively. The drought also resulted in severe water shortages that adversely affected domestic and livestock consumption requirements. Overally, the 1992 drought caused serious food insecurity at both the national and household levels of those that depended on agriculture. This constituted the context within which external support for drought relief was sought and received by the country.

PROJECT IDENTIFICATION

In February 1992, the Zambian President declared the drought a national disaster and an appeal for international relief was launched. As of April that year, the Food and Agriculture Organisation (FAO) and the World Food Programme (WFP) estimated that a total of 970,000 tonnes of cereals had to be brought into the country to avert starvation. It was as a result of these appeals that the international community, including Sweden, responded to the national problem. The international donors, looking at the problem as a regional catastrophe, moved in through a relief operation that covered most of southern Africa. Under the name of Drought Emergency in Southern Africa (DESA), the relief operation covered the ten Southern African Development Community (SADC) member states.

PROJECT DESIGN AND IMPLEMENTATION

The Swedish government became aware of the impending drought in early 1992 through its Development Cooperation Offices (DCOs) located in its embassies in the Southern African region. The Swedish International Development Agency (SIDA) responded positively and promptly to the drought signals by alerting authorities within its organisation as well as the UN system and NGOs about the magnitude of the problem. As one of the post-drought evaluations noted:

> SIDA acted both forcefully and on time to mobilise the necessary resources... In particular, [SIDA] organised studies of the logistics at an early stage and summoned the NGO representatives in Stockholm to brief them and encourage them to attend to this crisis. The local SIDA offices were very active in identifying components of aid. They entered into dialogue with the recipient governments and liaised with other bilateral donors and UN representatives... Before the UN appeal became official, [SIDA] plans were formed and decisions taken to reallocate bilateral funds at work.[79]

The above summary of SIDA's immediate response is confirmed by a brief look at how the Swedish government reacted to the crisis. Firstly, immediately SIDA established that a critical drought episode was imminent in the region, DCOs were given orders to monitor the situation in the affected countries. SIDA's division that is responsible for NGOs sent a mission to the region to assess its transport capacity in view of the planned shipments of food aid. This mission was followed by a study that examined southern Africa's transport constraints.[80] At the same time, SIDA formed the Drought Working Party that was mandated to monitor the developments in the region. At the international level, it was SIDA that alerted the UN Under-Secretary General for Humanitarian Affairs about the impending crisis. It was also SIDA that started the initiatives that resulted in the May 1992 donors' consultative meeting, chaired by the World Bank, with the aim of drumming up support for an international donor conference on southern Africa's drought relief. In specific terms, a total of SEK 115 million was given by Sweden to Zambia as drought relief. The grant focused principally on food and its transportation. Following an agreement with the Zambian government to re-allocate funds that were already committed under bilateral cooperation, Sweden mobilised SEK 66 million for food aid of which SEK 50 million covered ocean freight costs of yellow maize originating from the United States. A total of SEK 24.6 million was used to acquire the maize from the US. Smaller amounts of target food aid were also allocated. Table 7.1 shows the summary of Swedish aid support to the Zambian drought relief programme in 1992.

---

[79] Rundin, U. et al., 1993, p. 3.

[80] Sedin, B & S. Lööf, 1992.

Table 7.1. *Swedish aid to 1992 drought relief in Zambia and channels of distribution* (SEK '000)

Type of aid	Amount	Channel
Programme food aid		
Reallocation of bilateral funds	66,000	GRZ & USAID
Procurement of US maize	24,600	GRZ & USAID
Target food aid		
Procurement of tarpaulins	4,880	WFP/PAM
Water supply and infra-structure rehabilitation	3,000	UNICEF & GRZ
Groundnuts	2,700	WFP/PAM & GRZ
Production of millet & sorghum seed	400	GRZ/private producer

Source: Rundin, U. et al., *Evaluation of Swedish Support to the Drought Operations in Southern Africa*, Stockholm: SIDA, 1993, p. 35.

Overall, Sweden contributed 14% of Zambia's total drought support receipts from the international donor community. Another important aspect to note in Swedish aid assistance procedures during the DESA operations in Zambia is that it used three distinct channels of disbursements, namely, direct contributions to (a) the Zambian government; (b) the UN agencies, mainly the WFP; and (c) NGOs, mainly the Programme Against Malnutrition (PAM). SIDA entered into specific agreements with each organisation that received the drought relief funds. In principle, SIDA stipulated in such agreements that its procurement procedures should be followed. In practice, however, it was established that some of the executing agencies used their own rules. Such organisations as WFP, UNICEF and some NGOs had their own procurement procedures that they used instead of the Swedish ones.

Once the resources were received, actual expenditure was extended to such areas as food procurement; ocean shipping; land haulage; local level food distribution; rehabilitation of agriculture facilities; and general logistical and administrative expenses that included the process of identifying the target groups.

The organisational structure that was established to administrate the DESA in Zambia is outlined in Figure 7.1. At the national level, a number of organisational and delivery mechanisms were put in place to ensure effective utilisation of donor support and SIDA and WFP agreed in principle with such arrangements. First and foremost, the Zambian government, in collaboration with the principal donors, agreed to establish an action oriented and coordinated drought relief administrative structure. In this respect, the Central Statistical Office was appointed to house the Drought Impact Monitoring System (DIMS) that was established in mid-1992. DIMS was

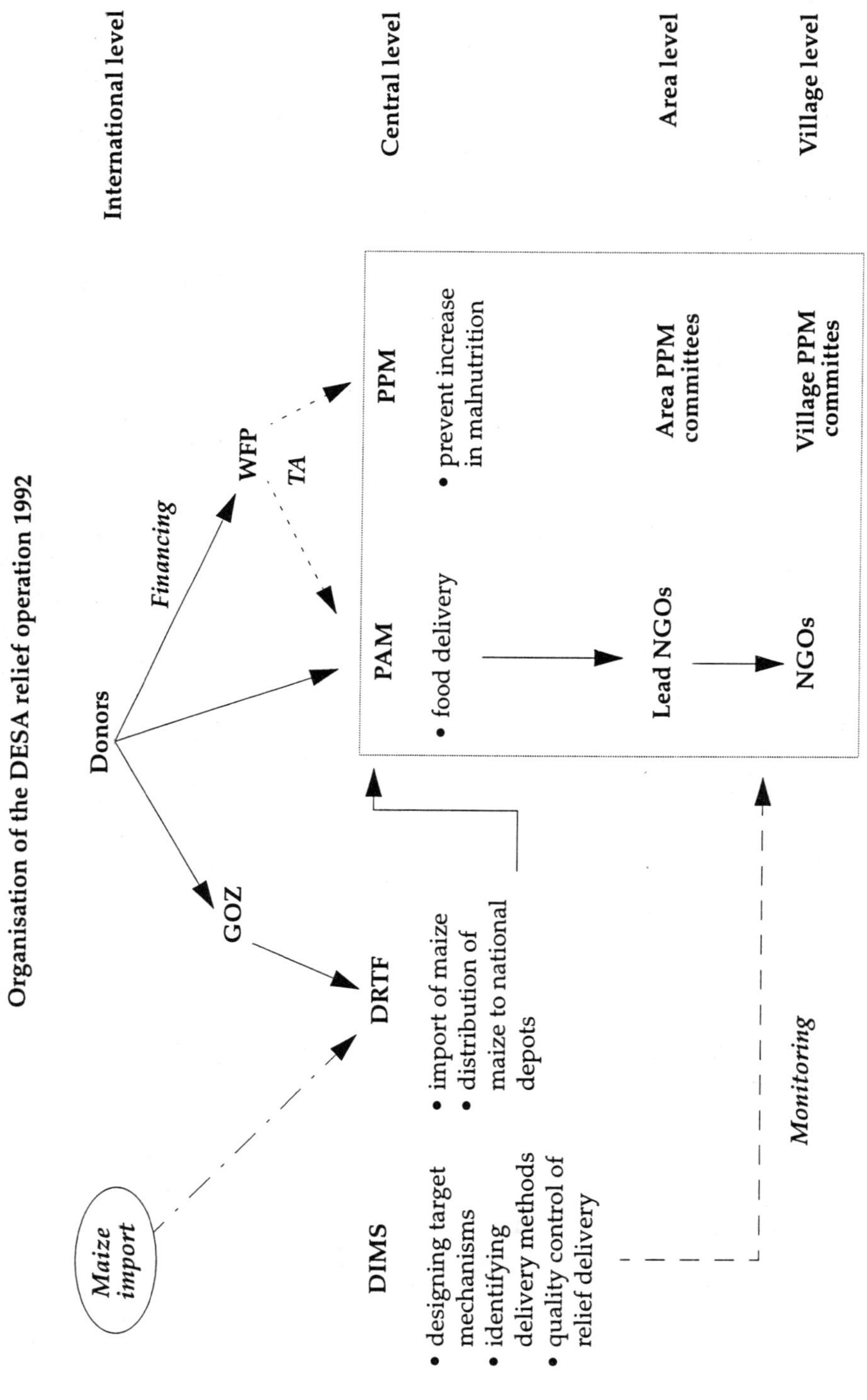

Figure 7.1. *Actors and relationships in the DESA operation*

financed mainly by FAO and UNICEF and its activities targeted at all the five provinces that were severely affected by drought. The systems' overall objective was to ensure that the drought relief programme identified the most efficient and effective methods of providing relief and assistance to drought affected areas by way of designing targeting mechanisms and triggering the delivery of relief or changes in the type of relief with a view to preventing distress and suffering.

In actual practice, DIMS aimed at assessing the level of malnutrition among the drought affected populations, particularly among the vulnerable groups. The system also assessed the degree to which agriculture-based households were able to maintain their productive assets (such as livestock, seed and tools) in a way that allowed them to have sustainable access to basic human needs. As an important component of DIMS, the system also included the assessment of the extent to which it was to form a basis of a more permanent system for monitoring household food security once the drought was over.

Against the above background and in recognition of the need to decentralise the management of aid relief in a way that involved the target community, an elaborate drought relief structure was designed that ran from the national to the village levels. Immediately the President declared the drought as a national disaster, the Drought Relief Task Force (DRTF) was created under the coordination of the Ministry of Agriculture. It was under the DRTF structure that the Ministries of Agriculture as well as Transport and Communications were mandated to import relief maize and to distribute it to national depots. The Ministry of Health, in turn, was given the task of distributing maize free of charge in areas that were classified as severely affected by the drought. Moreover, a number of sub-committees were established at the sub-regional levels to be in charge of drought administration especially in the fields of local resource mobilisation; logistics; internal distribution; hunger relief; animal health and disease control; water development; and agricultural credit management.

Still at the national level, the Ministry of Health initiated in April 1992 the Programme to Prevent Malnutrition (PPM) whose main aim was to arrest the increased malnutrition cases in drought-hit regions. Under the alternating chairmanship of the Ministers of Health and Agriculture, PPM membership included all relevant government ministries; WFP; and UN agencies. It was through PPM that the participation of NGOs in the task of distributing relief grain was sanctioned. Actual food relief distribution within Zambia began around July 1992 and PAM was the main NGO that was activated at the national level. This was an NGO that was specifically created for this purpose and received logistical support and guidance mainly from WFP. At the sub-national level, area PPM Committees were created in Zambia's drought belt that covered much of the southern half of the country. Once an area was targeted for relief, a lead NGO was chosen by the National

PPM/PAM Committee in conjunction with the Area PPM. Such an NGO, chosen on the strength of its local and grassroots level experience, became the implementing and coordinating agent of that particular area's drought relief activities. The NGOs included the Red Cross; churches; Oxfam; Development Aid from People to People (DAPP); etc.

It is noteworthy in the context of assessing the drought relief programme's effectiveness and sustainability that it was the Village PPM Committee that handled actual grain distributional tasks at the village level. The Village PPM Committees usually consisted of area chiefs; village elders and headmen; church elders; and NGO and local government representatives that were based in the catchment area. Three methods of grain distribution were employed at the village/community level, namely, commercial sales; Food-for-Work approach; and free food disbursement to the most needy.

PROGRAMME EFFECTIVENESS AND SUSTAINABILITY

The effectiveness the Swedish and WFP support to the drought operations in Zambia during 1992/93 could be judged at three different levels:

— the relief system's ability to deliver drought relief;

— the degree to which the process of disbursing drought relief has facilitated the building of institutional capacities needed for a more lasting and replicable effort in the event of another similar catastrophe;

— the extent to which the grassroots level recipients were allowed to participate in the project design and implementation in a way that facilitated the promotion of community participation in similar initiatives and/or efforts in future and especially upon the withdrawal of external support.

The above issues are examined below.

DROUGHT RELIEF DELIVERY

Generally speaking, drought relief operations in Zambia during 1992 have been hailed as a great success. Firstly, there were no reports of confirmed serious cases of starvation following the international community's positive response to the calls for assistance. By April 1992, FAO and WFP estimated that Zambia required a total of 970,000 tonnes of cereals for the impending crisis to be averted. Out of this estimate, the level of food vulnerability suggested that as much as 820,000 tonnes had to be in the form of food aid. By June 1993 when the relief operations came to an end, these figures were almost met. For example, according to the Ministry of Agriculture's Early Warning Unit, the country had by that time actually received a total of

896,000 tonnes of grain out of which roughly 670,000 tonnes were for food aid. While logistical constraints often delayed actual grain delivery to the remotest areas, particularly in the inaccessible border locations, a number of emergency operations averted an otherwise desperate situation. Moreover, no mass physical movement of people in search of food from the affected areas was reported. This was largely due to the decentralised system of delivery that allowed relief supplies to reach many remote villages. Thus, generally speaking, relief stocks were within a reasonable distance of the targeted beneficiaries.

Apart from the question of *availability* the issue of actual *access* was also attended to. Grain, when sold, was offered at subsidised and affordable prices. The other methods of relief, namely Food-for-Work and free distribution catered for the special categories of vulnerability. What the above state of affairs suggested was that the *immediate* reason for aid support (i.e. drought relief to avert starvation) was met to a considerable extent and this has generally been seen as one of the major success of the drought relief programme.

INSTITUTIONAL CAPACITY BUILDING AND COMMUNITY PARTICIPATION

Institutional capacity building and strengthening at the national and sub-national levels and the attendant community participation component are usually perceived to be important elements in the recipient's interpretation of aid effectiveness. This is largely due to the fact that, if programme or project sustainability is to be assured, the characteristic institutional and structural weaknesses of most delivery mechanisms have to be corrected.

Perhaps the most important success record of the donors' efforts in their relief operations during the 1992 drought is borders on the realisation that the drought relief programme's organisational structure provided a unique marriage of the donors, the government, the private sector, NGOs, and local communities themselves in actual planning and delivery of emergency activities. The decentralised involvement of all these diverse actors in the design and actual implementation and management of relief stocks had much to commend it. It is particularly noteworthy that community participation (at the grassroots level) in the relief effort also tended to minimise the traditional 'red tape' that is so characteristic of government-based and dominated delivery mechanisms. Besides, studies world-wide have revealed that the involvement of communities and extra-government agencies in the delivery of a service usually yields positive results. It has been established, for example, that communities and locally-based agencies that closely work with them tend to respond favourably and promptly to problems if and when they perceive themselves as the 'managers' of such interventions. This aspect is particularly crucial when looked at from the perspective of programme sustainability and, in the case of a drought situation, the ability of the process that is put in place to rehabilitate the production structures in a way that assures the long-term and sustainable solution to the problem of household food insecurity.

Similarly, another major success of the 1992 drought relief scheme was its potential to develop the local community through the Food-for-Work programme. In the areas where this was well-planned and coordinated, projects that benefited both the households (e.g. increased agricultural output due to the SIDA-supported seed distribution component and the clearing of fields) and the community at large (e.g. the development of irrigation systems, roads, clinics, etc.) were undertaken. In other words, the drought relief programme succeeded in both (a) averting the disaster of food insecurity at the household level and (b) creating a sustainable developmental framework that, if and when well re-oriented, should go well beyond the drought problem. Consequently, all the participants in the relief scheme, namely, the government; the donor community; PPM; PAM; NGOs; and the local communities agreed that PPM/PAM should continue their activities beyond the official date when drought relief came to an end (i.e. end of May 1993). Accordingly, as from June 1993, PPM/PAM activities have shifted from drought *relief* to post-drought *recovery*.

The effectiveness of the 1992 drought relief operations could further be confirmed by the degree to which the institutions and organisational structure that were created to perform this task have been retained for the purpose of post-recovery developmental activities. The reconstitution of the original objectives of PAM and DIMS is quite instructive in this regard. First, with respect to PAM, the government decided that this NGO structure should be retained during the post-drought period so that the organisation continues its assistance in the field of drought recovery. Consequently, "PAM is shifting its emphasis from emergency relief to a more development-oriented goal of post-drought recovery. PAM will operate as the coordinating agency throughout the country for the more than fifty NGOs that had participated in the PAM drought relief programme".[81]

With respect to DIMS, one notes that although this system was created to serve as a drought impact monitoring instrument, its mission has been reoriented into a much more permanent vulnerability monitoring system in the area of household food security, nutrition and health. During this drought recovery period, this monitoring system's main activities include the following:

— strengthening of the capacities of the Central Statistical Office and the National Food and Nutrition Commission with a view to establishing a policy and user-friendly data base as well as a geographic information system; and

81 SADCC, 1993 , p. 50.

— improving data dissemination systems in a way that facilitates a more frequent and direct dialogue between data producers, policy makers and implementers.

Overall, therefore, one of the major achievements of DESA activities in Zambia is their having facilitated a viable institutional structure that works towards the building of a sustainable and effective disaster preparedness capacity at the national and local levels. The role of NGOs is particularly important in this respect. Zambia decided at an early stage to use NGOs for the purpose of reaching the remote rural areas since they generally possess the ability to reach such parts because of their characteristic attribute of working closely with grassroots people. The success of the food distribution systems at this level is an important indicator of the merits, real and potential, of channelling donor resources not through the overly bureaucratic government channels but through the NGOs and the private sector. In a liberalised policy environment such as the one prevailing in Zambia today, this success story may point to the need to depart from the traditional channels of emergency relief to alternative delivery systems other than the government.

Although NGOs demonstrated certain limitations in their capacity such as their being generally ill-equipped to handle large quantities of relief food supplies, this may merely point to the need to target support in capacity building for these organisations. Notwithstanding this, one still observes a certain element of reluctance on the part of the Zambian government to encourage donors to deal directly with NGOs in drought relief operations. The reported sentiments of a government official in September 1994 in response to the 1994 drought relief exercise shed light on this:

> ... the decision by some donors to deal with NGOs would ... create problems for government. We have nothing against NGOs being used in the exercise but this is a national programme which we would like to control centrally because it is a sensitive issue. Government had planned a programme for each area but if several NGOs were used coordination of the exercise would be affected.[82]

What the above suggests is that there are still some camps within the government system that feel that centralised systems of delivery are appropriate.

THE AID RELATIONSHIP IN THE *DESA* OPERATION

The lessons learned from the DESA operation in terms of the aid relationship are quite instructive, in a positive sense. The whole operation was from the start built upon a far-reaching dialogue encompassing not only the traditional interface between donor and line ministry, but representatives of the

82 *Times of Zambia*, 26 September 1994, p. 1.

target communities as well. The organisation established for the purpose of distributing aid was decentralised and made extensive use of organisations outside the normal government apparatus. Thus, functioning interfaces were built up at the provincial, as well as the district and community levels. The DESA is a good, but rare, example of effective aid coordination within the government, as well as between the government and the different local organisations implementing the drought relief. The effectiveness of the DESA in terms of preventing starvation and death was high. It is difficult to say anything specific about the sustainability of the intervention. But one could hypothesise that as long as the organisational structure set up by DESA is maintained there will be a good preparedness to effectively handle future droughts in the country.

Chapter 8

Ground Water Development Project in Southern Province

BACKGROUND

Over the 1981–83 period, Zambia's Southern Province experienced an unbroken three-year drought which resulted in severe hardships for both humans and livestock. Due to this problem, the Zambian government established in Southern Province the Groundwater Development Project under its Rural Water Supply Programme. The government of Japan was requested to assist the programme with financial and technical support. This request received a positive response from Japan and its development agency, the Japan International Cooperation Agency, moved into Southern Province, a region whose principal preoccupation is subsistence and commercial agriculture.

PROJECT IDENTIFICATION AND DESIGN

The Southern Province Groundwater Development Project was supported mainly by JICA. Following the official request, the Japanese government, through JICA, sent a team to Zambia, headed by an engineer, to carry out a survey for 18 days in March/April 1985 with a view to establishing the magnitude of the problem and the level of possible support. The survey team held a series of discussions with government officials and undertook field investigations in the target area. Following the survey results, the government of Japan did further screening of the project request in Japan. This was in line with the standard Japanese grant aid procedures which stipulate that:

> ... after a request has been selected for consideration, a basic design study ... is carried out in order to formulate the project. This study is conducted by a survey team comprising Japanese government officials and experts from private consulting firms. They study the background, purpose, contents and effect of the development project concerned, the optimal scale of the project ... and local conditions to be taken into consideration in implementing the project.[83]

Following the screening process, the government of Japan undertook the first phase of the project in Southern Province in 1985. According to the

---

[83] JICA, 1986, p. 10.

'Minutes of Discussion' on the project signed in March 1985 between the Zambian and Japanese governments, the following items were specified as being required by the Zambian government as grant aid assistance:

— equipment;
— spares;
— construction of boreholes;
— training of the Department of Water Affairs (DWA) personnel on siting, boring, and installation of well materials; and
— advice on project organisation and planning.

Under a grant aid cooperation programme, JICA was to construct 102 deep wells for emergency relief. This first phase was undertaken and completed in 1987. Under similar conditions, the Zambian government requested Japan to provide a grant for Phase II of the same project in Southern Province, this time to cover 120 deep wells as well as to rehabilitate 100 wells that were malfunctioning. As in Phase I, JICA sent a Japanese study team for four weeks (March/April 1988). After the feasibility study, further screening was done in Japan. Upon the completion of this process, the Exchange of Notes (the agreement) was signed between the two governments covering a two and half year period.

In both Phases I and II of the project, the project objectives were as follows:

— to reduce the number of diseases related to insanitary drinking water;
— to minimise drought damage; and
— to stabilise the livelihood and social conditions in the rural areas by supplying safe, reliable drinking water throughout the year to rural residents.

The project sites were in the seven districts of Southern Province, namely, Mazabuka; Choma; Namwala; Gwembe; Monze; Kalomo; and Livingstone.

PROJECT IMPLEMENTATION

The Southern Province Groundwater Development Project was typical Japanese grant aid support in which, according to the official standard procedures:

> ... the procurement of goods and services is made in accordance with the contract between a Japanese firm and the government of the recipient country. The exchange of notes stipulates that the procurement can be made only in Japan and the recipient country.[84]

Consequently, the project was subcontracted to a Japanese company called Pacific Consultants International Ltd. after it won the tender that was open

[84] JICA, 1986, op. cit., p. 8.

exclusively to Japanese companies only and conducted in Japan. The roles of respective actors in project implementation were clearly specified. On the Zambian government side, the responsible agency for project implementation was the Ministry of Agriculture and Water Development while construction works were assigned to DWA. According to the project's design, the Zambian side provided the required personnel for project implementation, in addition to materials not provided by Japan. Additionally, DWA was expected to conduct periodic inspections, repairs, maintenance and management of the completed wells in both Phases I and II of the project. Moreover, the project design provided that "DWA shall provide the residents with the guidance necessary for them to develop a sanitary environment and for establishing a well maintenance and management system which residents, as a village unit, will be able to participate in and be responsible for".[85]

As an additional responsibility of DWA, the maintenance and management of well facilities were expected to be undertaken by each DWA's District Officer who is under the supervision of the manager of DWA's Provincial Office. The identification of borehole sites to be drilled and rehabilitated was also the responsibility of DWA particularly during Phase II of the project.

On the Japanese side, the Japanese contractor (Pacific Consultants International Ltd) was assigned the responsibility of acquiring and supplying equipment and materials for the project. Such equipment included vehicles; testing instruments; workshop and maintenance tools; deep well hand pumps; materials for the construction of deep wells; and spare parts for the equipment. In addition, JICA through the contractor, provided technical services for construction work. Such services included the dispatch of contractor's staff (mainly engineers); procurement of local materials; execution of on-the-job training for locals; technical services for the construction of new borehole facilities as well as for the rehabilitation of existing borehole facilities; and the preparation of monthly progress reports. As an integral part of the Japanese contractor's responsibility, Pacific Consultants International extended basic drilling techniques to DWA personnel during Phases I and II of the project.

PROJECT EFFECTIVENESS AND SUSTAINABILITY

The effectiveness and sustainability of the JICA-supported Groundwater Development Project could be measured at three levels, namely:

— the degree to which the original immediate objectives were realised;

[85] JICA, 1988.

- the appropriateness of project identification, design and implementation mechanisms; and
- the extent to which there were resources, both human and financial and at the national and local levels, that would make project survival beyond JICA support assured.

These criteria of project effectiveness and sustainability are discussed below.

REALISATION OF OBJECTIVES

When examined purely from the technical angle, the project target/goals achieved a certain level of success during both Phases I and II. When Phase I came to an end in 1987, the target number of boreholes were constructed and this evidently relieved some 300,000 inhabitants of Southern Province from drought- and insanitariness-related problems. The grant aid for Phase II envisages the construction of 120 boreholes and the rehabilitation of 100 disused wells. The JICA drilling teams, through Pacific Consultants International, supplied equipment and constructed 32 new boreholes. They also rehabilitated 40 malfunctioning wells. In addition to this and in accordance with the contract stipulation, the JICA contractor provided technical guidance, advice and construction supervision to the Zambian project team within DWA. Some Zambians were also sent to Japan for training to facilitate a smooth handover of the project tasks to DWA by JICA upon the end of Japanese assistance.

As per plan, the JICA team handed over the equipment and materials (including the warehouse workshop) to DWA that was expected to complete the construction of 88 new boreholes and the rehabilitation of 60 malfunctioning ones from the Phase I work. After this process, JICA withdrew from Southern Province altogether and moved into Phase III that covered Lusaka and Central Provinces.[86] Notwithstanding the above positive aspects of the project, there are no indications that the project designers possessed clear monitoring procedures and mechanisms as well as indicators for success-cum-effectiveness. The principal objective of the project was to reduce the number of diseases related to insanitary drinking water (e.g. diarrhoeal ailments) so that the livelihood and social conditions in the targeted areas are stabilised. In this regard, the supply of water points is not an end in itself but a means to the realisation of the above objective. Hence, unless the water infrastructure provision translated into positive attainment of the stated objectives, the project's effectiveness from the recipient standpoint would remain unsatisfactory.

This study established that the project designers neither developed indicators for measuring the realisation of a marked reduction in water-related

[86] Phase III of JICA support to Zambia is not part of this case study.

diseases nor were there clearly stipulated monitoring procedures pertaining to the actual utilisation of the water points by the target communities in Southern Province. To the extent that this shortcoming in project planning/ design compromised the actual determination of project success, it meant that the *real* impact of the project (hence, its effectiveness) on the target population could not be readily established.

PROJECT DESIGN AND IMPLEMENTATION

The Groundwater Development Project was conceived by the Zambian government as a response to the pressure exerted by drought conditions. Southern Province is one of the main maize growing regions in the country. The province also supplies the largest proportion of Zambian beef requirements. Thus, apart from the adverse effects of drought conditions on the inhabitants of the province, the consequences of this calamity in that province were felt throughout the country. The Japanese government's positive and prompt response to the Zambian appeal for assistance was, thus, timely. In this regard, the project served the real needs of the target populations and beyond.

Notwithstanding the above, a number of project design weaknesses were established during this study. Firstly, the identification of the target population's felt needs was done at a very high level in a process that almost exclusively depended on technical experts to determine what was required and feasible. Hence, project viability and feasibility were perceived as being determined chiefly by the technical and economic soundness of the proposal and little effort was made to understand and appreciate the socio-economic preferences of the target population. In this respect, community participation was evidently alien to the project design, implementation and monitoring, let alone evaluation. There were reported consultations of local chiefs by the technical teams on the locations of water points while the actual beneficiaries' input at this stage was not solicited.

Secondly, at the implementation level, the beneficiary community was once more marginalised under conditions where it was DWA that was expected to handle even simple water point preventive maintenance. Under conditions where the beneficiaries were not taught even the most basic knowledge of equipment maintenance as an integral part of project aid support, the water points were generally perceived as 'JICA' property whose maintenance was none of their business. This approach to project planning and implementation adversely affected the chances of project sustainability and effectiveness. Due to the limited capacity and resource constraints of DWA, a number of wells malfunctioned shortly after they were constructed because of handpump breakdowns or drying up of wells. Thus, at the beginning of Phase II, at least 100 handpump wells needed to be rehabilitated. It was, therefore, not surprising that out of the 886 water points in Southern

Province that were surveyed by DWA's Community Management Monitoring Unit (CMMU) from October to December 1993, 33% were not in use and the most cited reason for this in cases of boreholes with pumps related to component problems (90% of the reported cases).[87]

Another dimension of the problem concerns the anticipated level of input from DWA vis-à-vis its institutional capacity to handle effectively its part of project implementation. In contrast to the initial stages of the NORAD support to Western Province Water Supply Programme and the FINNIDA-supported ZEMP, this project was fully integrated into the government system right from the beginning and it depended quite significantly on government personnel occupying line positions. While such an integration with the recipient institution is desirable, the main problem with the JICA-supported project was not that it operated outside the government framework. Rather, the weaknesses seem to be the exact opposite: it overly depended on an ill-equipped government system for both project implementation and monitoring. Under the project plan, it was the responsibility of DWA to provide all the personnel needed to implement the project under the guidance of the Japanese engineers/experts. In addition to this, maintenance of water points as well as the teaching of the community on sanitary methods of utilising the wells (an aspect introduced in Phase II of the project) were also the total responsibility of DWA.

The experience of the two phases demonstrated that the capacity of DWA to undertake the above responsibilities was quite low. Because DWA personnel's technical skills were inadequate to operate the Japanese technology that was brought in, serious anomalies resulted. The sentiments expressed by JICA with respect to its experience with Phase I of the project are quite revealing in this respect:

> Zambian engineers have learned the basic techniques of borehole drilling and equipment operations that were passed on to them by the Japanese engineers who were dispatched under the Phase I Project. However, the consumption rates of drilling tools among Zambian engineers are high and their capability to apply the techniques to different types of geological conditions, drilling troubles, and other unexpected but related problems remain insufficient ... Frequent breakdowns of high-pressure air compressors, DTH hammers, and drilling machines occurred ... due to the drilling team's insufficient technique application capabilities, improper operations, or equipment overuse ... Thus, it will be necessary for the Japanese engineers assigned to the Project to provide the transfer of techniques to update the Zambian engineers' technical levels.[88]

What the above revelation suggests is that the problems encountered at the operational level were mainly due to improper project design particularly with respect to the project's overdependence on inexperienced local per-

---

[87] DWA/CMMU, 1994.

[88] Pacific Consultants International, 1990.

sonnel since there were no arrangements to train them prior to their engagement in the activities that demanded trained skills.

A related problem concerns DWA's inability to conduct periodic inspections, repairs, maintenance and adequate management of the completed wells especially in the absence of community participation. While this is traditionally the function of the recipient to ensure that what is acquired through donor support is efficiently maintained, the financial limitations of most government departments ought be to recognised. The Zambian government is usually called upon to meet the recurrent costs of a multitude of grant-aided projects. Consequently, it has to allocate a substantial financial outlay as well as manpower resources to such projects as 'counterpart' contribution. As a result, the multiplicity of donors whose operations are usually not effectively coordinated has placed a considerable functional strain on the ill-equipped, weak, and overstretched government administrative and implementation systems. This phenomenon significantly explains the government's general failure to meet its share of the cost of many donor-aided projects particularly when, as is usually the case, government contributions to donor assisted programmes/projects have to come from extra-budgetary sources.

The above generalisations seem to hold true for the two phases of the Japan-aided Groundwater Development Project in Southern Province. Firstly, DWA's budget covers mainly routine recurrent expenses and very little is usually earmarked for large scale maintenance and rehabilitation of equipment. Project monitoring by DWA is also checked by inadequate transport for its personnel. Consequently, an alarming number of wells that were constructed during Phase I of the project became malfunctional by the end of that phase.

Secondly, there is little evidence suggesting that a proper feasibility study to establish the appropriate model for wells and pumps was undertaken. The high failure rates of boreholes, mainly due to silting, and frequent breakdowns of pumps suggested that little attention was given to these technical details particularly during the earlier phase of the project. This seems to endorse some of the general concerns in the debate about the appropriateness of the technology that is often transferred under grant aid. As the 1986 UNDP report on the role of technical cooperation in Zambia observed:

> ... the professional background of foreign advisers is often predicated upon the existence of sophisticated support systems which are unavailable locally. People used to such environment are often unable to re-think and simplify professional solutions. They tend to imitate structures, therefore, which do not last—sometimes the project functions only while the expatriate is in post.[89]

---

89 UNDP, 1986.

A related aspect of the above problem with respect to the *modus operandi* of Japanese grant aid refers to the earlier stated conditionality. Under Japanese grant aid, (a) all equipment had to be sourced from Japan, save for a few materials that were available locally; and (b) the tender for project implementation was open to Japanese firms only. The consequence of these conditionalities was that Zambia's special requirements had to coincide with what the Japanese technical assistance personnel could offer otherwise the project's chances of effectiveness and sustainability remained threatened. Considering the limited exposure to Zambia's local conditions by the Japanese experts and the questionable ability of the local engineers to efficiently operate Japanese equipment (resulting in the reported poor equipment handling), the above conditionalities evidently contradicted the recipient government's expectations.

HUMAN, FINANCIAL AND TECHNOLOGICAL RESOURCES

The sustainability of the Southern Province Groundwater Development Project beyond the withdrawal of Japanese external support is largely contingent on the availability within the country of the necessary human, financial and technological resources at the national level. Beginning with the human resources consideration, it is noteworthy that the Japanese grant aid for the project included the provision for the training of indigenous experts/counterparts so that, upon the withdrawal of technical assistance personnel, these people took over. Indeed, when the Japanese engineers withdrew from the project, Zambian professionals took over and completed the remaining part of Phase II of the project activities. In this regard, it could be argued that the project has provided for the development of institutional capacity at this level.

When consideration of long-term sustainability is made, one recognises as the major weakness the project's failure to build into its implementation plan aspects of community participation. During Phase I of the project, no attempt was made towards involving the beneficiaries in the planning and implementation of activities. Local people were neither involved in the siting of the well points nor in the actual construction and maintenance of these. As a result, the reported low level of 'JICA' borehole utilisation in some parts of the Province seemed to have reflected the degree to which socio-cultural considerations of the target communities were allowed to be overshadowed by technical aspects. The delegation to DWA of the total responsibility of maintenance and management of well facilities also overlooked the fact that minimum training on how to handle these tasks effectively was required on the part of government personnel. DWA personnel also required skills in the enhancement of participatory methodologies and mechanisms if their task of educating the community on hygienic methods of well utilisation was to be effective. Community education that is similar to what is built into the NORAD-supported Western Province Water Supply Programme, under its Community Education and Participation component is of direct relevance in this regard. Without basic knowledge in participatory methodologies, the DWA personnel performed quite poorly in the well point maintenance and management. As the JICA report that reflected on the experiences of the project's Phase I acknowledged:

> ... a substantial number of malfunctioning wells underwent repairs each year but ... in a very short time, they began malfunctioning again. Furthermore, even when minor damage or operational problems occurred, the wells would either be put back into use after makeshift repairs or would continue to be used without repairs or servicing. As a result, a number of wells became completely inoperable.[90]

Against the above experience, it could be concluded that the maintenance of well facilities and the transfer to the communities of repair and preventive maintenance skills should have been an integral and important component of the Japanese grant aid to the project in order to enhance its effectiveness and sustainability.

It is noteworthy that the experience of Phase I of the project gave JICA and the Zambian government the opportunity to reflect seriously on the low level of the integration of the beneficiary community in well maintenance and repairs. Consequently, it was agreed that the following interventions should constitute an important aspect of the project management in future:

— selecting suitable persons from each village and impart well maintenance and management techniques to them in order for them to qualify as well inspectors;

— establishing a well maintenance and management system in each village, township and district;

— providing guidance to beneficiary communities on how to increase their awareness of public health, water quality, sanitation, etc.;

— engaging in publicising the project unlike during Phase I when local people saw a 'Japanese team' moving into the drilling sites and making a borehole without the community having prior knowledge of the arrival of the 'foreigners' and the purpose of their mission; and

— conducting periodic inspections of well points.

The creation of the Community Management and Monitoring Unit (CMMU) at DWA is equally significant as this is the unit that is expected to address some of the vexing issues pertaining to rural water supply and sanitation in the whole country, including Southern Province. With proper human and financial support, CMMU should be able to provide the backstopping needed particularly in the area of the development of participatory methodolo-

90 JICA, 1988, p. 259.

gies that aim at improving community involvement in project planning, implementation and management. Equally significant towards project effectiveness and sustainability is the reported initiative by JICA[91] to appoint an expert on community mobilisation to be stationed at DWA with a view to strengthening its capacity in the area of mobilising the communities into appreciating community-based management and maintenance systems.

THE AID RELATIONSHIP IN THE JAPANESE SUPPORTED WATER AND SANITATION PROGRAMME

The experiences of this project offer many important insights into the difficulties of establishing an effective aid relationship. It combines many of the experiences found in the ZEMP and the Western Province water project. The design of the project was very much a joint undertaking between Zambia and Japan but at the level of the line ministry only. The design reflected a pronounced engineering approach to water provision—the project was about drilling bore holes. There were no attempts to situate the project within the social, cultural and economic context of the target communities. The aid relationship never extended down to these levels. The mode of operation of the project depended on a division of labour between the responsible government authorities and the JICA, but never really involved the communities. This limitation to the aid relationship had, as it turned out, a negative impact on the effectiveness of the support.

The duties of DWA in particular were quite extensive and the effectiveness of the project was quite dependent on DWA's ability to fulfil its obligations. One major weakness of the NORAD supported activities in Western Province, in the early stages, was a lack of integration with the government structure. In the Southern Province it was the other way around. A major weakness of the JICA-supported project was perhaps too much integration and reliance on the existing institutional and financial capacities of DWA. The existence of many donor projects requiring a "counterpart" contribution from the government highlights the need for aid coordination in order to make the most efficient use of the few resources the government has at its disposal. Add to this the fact that the communities were never really mobilised to maintain the installed water points. It is striking that the government never really voiced any concerns about its limitations for fulfilling its part of the deal. Again, we see a conflict pattern of withdrawal and suppression.

91 During interviews with A.C. Daka, Technical Cooperation Secretary, JICA-Zambia Office, 8 September 1994.

Chapter 9

Aid Administration and Coordination

INTRODUCTION

The case studies have, among many things, brought out the issue of coordination as a common denominator. A key feature of the aid relationship in Zambia seems to be a lack of coordination of various aid programmes and projects, among the donors themselves, and in particular within the government. coordination is, however, a phenomenon which everybody talks about and it almost always carries a positive connotation. It is good to coordinate: it is a sign of efficiency and collaboration. Still, one is often left with the feeling that not too many of its proponents have thought through what it actually means to coordinate. Let us therefore start by defining the phenomenon of coordination:

> To coordinate means to place or arrange things in proper position relative to each other and to the system of which they form parts—to bring into proper and combined order as parts of a whole. It means, in essence, to bring about some kind of order. Coordination may consist of a number of things of equal rank or of a number of actions and processes properly combined.[92]

What is the purpose of coordination? Generally, it is probably understood that coordination is a good way of avoiding a waste of scarce resources. Coordination is a tool for better decision-making. Translated into different decision-making situations one finds that coordination is needed when an organisation will make better decisions if it knows what other and related organisations are planning to do. Coordination is also useful where an organisation depends on decisions from another organisation to do something. Finally, coordination is needed when a number of organisations need to take decisions jointly. Coordination is not one tool, but many. They can be formal or informal, centralised or decentralised, and any combination among them, The following small matrix illustrates the possibilities.

The fact that the issue of coordination has become a permanent feature of the aid effectiveness debate is a good indication of how little has been achieved, and how difficult it is to achieve anything. The obstacles to coordination are many, and sometimes of such a magnitude that it should not come as a surprise that so little by way of effective coordination actually takes place in aid.

---

92 Forss, K., O. Saasa & J. Carlsson, 1995, p. 38.

Figure 9.1 *Coordination tools*

	Formal	*Informal*
Centralised	Instruction and orders	Liaison posts
		Action groups
		Committees
		Board representation
Decentralised	Standardisation of: skills, procedures, timing, input and output	Personal contacts and communication

Source: Forss, K., O. Saasa & J. Carlsson, *A Study of Coordination in the Zambian Education Sector. With a Focus on International Development Cooperation*. Stockholm: SIDA, January 1995, p. 42.

What makes aid coordination so difficult? Forss (1995) lists six of the most common obstacles involved. Some of them can be easily rectified, while others concern fundamental aspects of the aid relationship.

First, coordination is facilitated if there is a common set of values and norms concerning the purpose of the activities. In other words, if there is no common goal, and a lack of vision about the desired outcome then there is really no one interested in coordination. Second, coordination requires that information is available. For actors to take decisions they need to know what others in the system are doing. Third, if the involved parties employ widely different administrative systems and procedures, coordination becomes difficult. Fourth, there may very well be "hidden" objectives of the parties. Their expressed intentions for undertaking a certain activity may not be the real ones. Coordination can become a threat to the possibilities of the parties to realise their "true" objectives. Fifth, everybody likes to be recognised for their contribution and to get recognition for some special good deed they have done. It is not always part of human behaviour wanting to share this with others. The last obstacle concerns the transparency and accountability of decision-making structures. When responsibilities are diluted and the processes of work are unclear or hidden, then coordination becomes almost impossible.

In the last section of this chapter we shall return to a discussion of the relevance of these obstacles for aid coordination, and see to what extent they are connected to the quality of the aid relationship. Before then, we shall review the kind of coordination that characterises Zambia today.

AID COORDINATION IN ZAMBIA—THE REALITY

Our analysis of donor involvement in Zambia's development has revealed a diversity of external organisations and agencies, both bilateral and multilateral. The most crucial aspect in this regard is the realisation that a diversity of donors often find themselves involved in the support of the same sector or sub-sector, a phenomenon that suggests the need for some form of collaboration and/or harmonisation of their support initiatives. Our case studies have revealed that, in the water sector, NORAD, JICA and the Netherlands have provided financial and technical assistance. Similarly, the education sector has demonstrated an enormous capacity to attract donor funding. Apart from SIDA and FINNIDA that have special education sector support programmes and that have collaborated in ZEMP, such multilateral and bilateral donors as the World Bank, the British Council/ODA; the European Union; the African Development Bank; NORAD; JICA; and UNICEF have all continued to play strategic roles in the development of Zambia's education sector. Donor support is also received at the more general level of balance of payments support as demonstrated earlier.

The above state of affairs clearly demonstrates the need for aid coordination at different levels. The justification for this process does not end here. It is equally important to recognise how wasteful uncoordinated donor activities could be. The absence of coordination between aid agencies and between these bodies and the host government tends to perpetuate the problem of duplication of efforts, thus, complicating the aid management function of government. This assumption is founded on the understanding that the government (and, indeed, donors themselves) would be availed of a good opportunity to make informed decisions if and when they are familiar with what others are doing in the same fields. For example, coordination allows participants in the same field to learn from each other's successes and mistakes for the purpose of improving overall aid effectiveness. To take the two case studies of water aid as an illustration, one finds that if JICA's Groundwater Development project in Southern Province had tried to learn from NORAD's early mistakes in its support to the Western Province Water Supply and Sanitation Programme, the former could have made a much better use of its aid. Thus, as the NORAD Resident Representative in Zambia lamented in 1987:

> ... we made serious mistakes in Western Province water development programme five years ago ... We rectified these problems. The Japanese were involved in another province in a similar programme but made even worse mistakes than us. They could not learn from our earlier mistakes because of lack of ... coordination of our activities.[93]

Equally important, coordination allows partners in the same field to synchronise and properly sequence their actions. For example, in the absence of adequate and properly timed coordination, donors in Zambia tend to operate outside the framework of government planning and budget circles. Similarly, in the absence of meaningful coordination between donor pledges and the budgeting process, the usually agreed counterpart funds that are

[93] Jacob Storos, personal interview, 20 May 1987 as quoted in Saasa, O., 1987, p. 66.

expected to complement donor resources often have to come from extra-budgetary sources, if at all they are made available. In other words, when and if the government negotiations with, and receipt of commitments from, donors come after the national budget has been released, the integration of donor resources in the government budgetary and planning process becomes difficult, a phenomenon that has the propensity to allow donor resources to be administered not necessarily within the framework of state priorities.

Against the above background, to what extent is there effective aid coordination and management in Zambia? For analytical convenience, aid coordination in Zambia can be examined at the three different levels, namely:

— coordination within the national/government system;

— coordination between the government system and the donors); and

— coordination among donors.

In the context of the above three categories, aid coordination could also be examined at the national, sectoral and project/implementation levels. These categories are examined in the next section.

COORDINATION WITHIN GOVERNMENT

The need for aid coordination within the national system is founded on the premise that the various government and non-governmental organs that receive and utilise external assistance should operate under a functioning institutional framework within which such resources are effectively and efficiently managed and used for the intended purposes. In a situation where such a policy or organisational framework is non-existent, the tendency has been for donors to declare a 'vote of no confidence' in the system and on grounds of effectiveness, they often opted to operate around the established government structures.

To avoid the above state of affairs, host governments often establish institutional arrangements as well as dialogue or consultative mechanisms within the state system itself that govern or foresee the aid coordination functions. Strictly speaking, however, the Zambian government has up to now failed to establish a well-functioning, well-understood, and credible institutional framework at the national (i.e. macro) level within which aid is received, administered, utilised, monitored and its effectiveness evaluated. The ordinary administrative structure of the government encompasses three major levels—the central, the provincial and the district levels. Theoretically all these levels have clear functions in planning, executing and evaluating different government activities. Needless to say that effective coordination among these levels is the first requirement for basic aid coordination to take place. In most of the our case studies this does not work the way it was intended. Too often provincial and district levels are simply bypassed by decisions taken at the central level. The DESA case, on the other hand, represents an example of where administrative structures, at various levels, are effectively integrated with each other and where coordination seems to have worked rather well.

Attempts by the government to coordinate aid are currently being undertaken at the macro level only. A number of different and functionally disjointed wings of the state are occupied with this task. Presently, the National Commission for Development Planning (NCDP), operating under the Office of the President and spatially separate from the Ministry of Finance, is theoretically in charge of the task of aid coordination and monitoring. In practice, while considerable volumes of donor funds are routinely cleared via NCDP, mainly through its Division of Economic Cooperation, one still observes that the management of debt and the task of negotiating loans is usually done by the Ministry of Finance and the Bank of Zambia (i.e. the central bank).

An effort is presently ongoing to try to link external assistance to the government's planning and budgeting process. This effort is not being done by NCDP which is said to be in charge of mobilising, programming, monitoring and coordinating external assistance. Rather, this is the responsibility of the Ministry of Finance and the central bank. It is noteworthy, however, that this important process is currently being hampered by a number of institutional, organisational and human capacity weaknesses such as:

- insufficient collaboration and harmonisation between the arms of government that are charged with aid management, on the one hand, and its ultimate users, on the other;
- well-trained and experienced manpower deficiencies and equipment shortages; and
- absence of dependable data bases that show the magnitude and types of aid flows.

The lack of effective aid coordination within the government has become a concern of some donors. They have recognised the seriousness of the above structural weaknesses and have shown willingness to assist in building the government's institutional capacity. For example, since 1985, the United Nations Development Programme (UNDP) has provided advisory services to the government in the area of aid coordination and data collection. Through the National Technical Cooperation Assessments and Programmes (NATCAP) exercise that started in 1986, UNDP attempts to correct some weaknesses at the national level in the area of effective use of technical cooperation.

In addition to the above initiatives at the national level, the Technical Cooperation Management and Coordination Unit has been established at NCDP with tasks that include:

- overseeing the implementation of the technical cooperation policy and programme;
- preparing a rolling technical cooperation programme;
- adjusting and implementing guidelines on technical cooperation policy statement; and
- collecting and analysing data on technical cooperation requirements at both sectoral and inter-sectoral levels.[94]

Other donors are also involved in the process of strengthening the government capacity in aid coordination and management. The World Bank-administered Technical Assistance Project was started in 1991 and includes among its activities the support for a Resident Advisor on aid coordination and mobilisation. Generally, donors have acknowledged that

> ...the strengthening of government capacity in aid management and coordination will widen government ownership and develop its leadership role and that this is expected to have an important value-added dimension in terms of sound implementation, enhanced impact and improved development cooperation towards sustainable results.[95]

Let us then return to our matrix, Figure 9.1, and see in what box we can place the existing government system for aid coordination. The Zambian state administrative system is principally located in the box where coordination is centralised and formal. For a number of reasons, this system has not proved functional and we can see a gradual shift towards creating new structures, organisational units, for aid coordination. These are mainly centralised organs, with formalised functions. Still, however, their actual authority and functioning in relation to, for example, line ministries and to each other remains somewhat unclear.

DONOR-HOST COUNTRY COORDINATION

Coordination between the donor agency or agencies, on the one hand, and the government, on the other, should not be seen as a substitute for coordination that ought to take place within the government system itself. Rather, donor–host country coordination is important to the extent that it facilitates the national system having a more informed picture of the nature and extent of external support and using such knowledge to strengthen both its definition and redefinition of external involvement as well as consolidating its aid management capacity through an in-depth knowledge of what the donor does. By closely monitoring through, say, consultative meetings with donors, the government's seriousness of purpose would be revealed, itself an important catalyst to increased and continued donor support.

94 UNDP, 1995, p. 24.

95 Ibid, p. 24.

Likewise, without meaningful mechanisms of coordination between donors and the host government, duplication of effort is likely to emerge since donor priorities and preferences should not always be assumed to coincide with those of the state particularly under conditions where government policy is not clearly and coherently defined and articulated. Under such conditions, donors are given an exaggerated latitude to set their own standards and operational procedures that may not always conform to government expectations. Moreover, the existence of a multiplicity of donor procedures and demands could easily generate a functional strain on an already ill-equipped and overstretched bureaucracy whose absorptive capacity is admittedly weak. In the absence of an effective central coordination system, a number of sectoral committees have been established in the country that are largely bilateral in composition and which attempt to provide a forum for the exchange of views between the government and the respective donors. Such committees are usually composed of both government officials and representatives of donor agencies. The intention here is generally to facilitate close and joint monitoring of the developments in the respective programmes or projects that receive donor funding.

Notwithstanding the good intentions of such coordination or steering committees, a number of weaknesses still affect the effectiveness of a number of them. For example, although government and donor representatives on the committees are often quite senior people, there is a general tendency of sending junior colleagues to represent them during meetings. Even worse, poor attendance, particularly from the government side, has adversely minimised the effectiveness of coordination as decisions are often taken in the absence of qualified representation. Apart from coordination through the project committee system that assumes a multilateral form, the government also conducts annual joint reviews of a bilateral nature with respective donors. The purpose of these annual talks is to plan for new activities and review ongoing and completed ones. Theoretically, they should offer the government an opportunity to use its knowledge of what other donors are doing to avoid duplication of efforts. To what extent this takes place remains an open question.

One aspect that the preceding analysis suggests is that while there has been considerable lower level coordinating mechanisms through the proliferation of project committees, the link between the donors and the government at the "national" level is still weak. This should be considered a serious constraint since, ideally, effective coordination ought to take place at all the three levels, namely, national, sectoral and project. It is at the "national" level where the broad policy framework and the ranking of the country's priorities are undertaken. The competing needs and requirements of the various sectors and sub-sectors are identified and ranked at this level. It is at the "ministry" level where more specific sectoral priorities are defined and where coordinating committees that focus on specific sub-sectors draw their frames of reference. At the "project" level, one finds technical committees that are involved with the actual details of implementation.

Lastly, to strengthen the aid coordination function at the sectoral level, there is need to strengthen ministries' capacities by, inter alia, equipping them with the needed resources (technical and financial) so that they can generate the vital information required for effective coordination and planning. Additionally, as the *Focus on Learning* policy document argued for education,

> ... the technical aid office within the education sector needs to be much more highly developed so that it can negotiate competently with donors on projects and programmes, within the overall framework of agreed priorities; respond to the needs of donors for comprehensive information on the education system; monitor and evaluate the foreign aid inflows and the impact of that aid on the planned development of education; and advise more senior officers and other partners in education on all matters pertaining to aid.[96]

It is noteworthy that, at a multilateral level, the Zambian government uses the annual Consultative Group (CG) meeting as one of the principal mechanisms to facilitate aid mobilisation and coordination.

How shall we characterise the present type of donor–host country coordination taking place in Zambia? Returning again to Figure 9.1, the tools used are found in the upper right box. They are centralised and largely informal. Coordination takes place through committees, action groups, liaison posts etc. However, our case studies suggest that government bodies at the provincial and district levels tend to become marginalised in this coordination process.

COORDINATION AMONG DONORS

There are no formalised multilateral mechanisms of coordination among donors in Zambia. Notwithstanding this, quite regular, albeit informal, meetings and exchange of information among donors are observable. While informal consultative arrangements, being largely "ad hoc", are often more effective in arriving at some loose form of consensus among donors as to how they should cooperate and collaborate for a common good, one ought to recognise the limitations of this system of coordination. In particular, the absence of formalised procedures for discussing and reporting issues and decisions under the system of informal consultations means that such decisions are not binding to the parties involved since a "voluntarist" approach is adopted. It also means that there is no obligation for any donor in the sector to attend such meetings especially if it is felt that there are deep rooted conflicts of interest whether with respect to participating donors' priorities or just merely with regard to preferred procedures. While there is no evi-

[96] GRZ, *Focus on Learning*, 1992, p. 133.

dence suggesting that this is a problem at present, one can still raise the question regarding the degree to which the decisions of such informal coordination meetings filter their way to the other important actor in the aid coordination interface, namely, the government. Whether the government always needs to know the internal consultations among its donor partners is open to debate. What seems obvious, nevertheless, is that mechanisms that enhance the effective flow and exchange of information on aid management improve project implementation and sustainability, in addition to the promotion of systemic transparency.

Notwithstanding the above, there is a general feeling among donor agencies that the responsibility of coordinating donor activities should lie first and foremost on the shoulders of government. While recognising the importance of harmonising their activities and aid administrative procedures, donors generally argued that they are answerable to different constituencies with different aid policy and management procedures as well as varying priorities and strategies. While common grounds are many, it is generally argued that their allegiance is mainly to their respective governments and parliaments and, thus, their room for manoeuvre with respect to procedural issues tends to be circumscribed by headquarters. In this respect, it is generally felt that the onus is mainly with the recipient government to provide an institutional framework within which divergent—and sometimes conflicting—donor activities are coordinated and harmonised in a way that meets its set goals and priorities. This does not, however, imply that donors have no role in coordination enhancement. To the contrary, an effort among donors to agree amongst themselves regarding common grounds could go a long way in assisting the recipient government in its effort towards effective aid coordination. It is also the donor agencies that are better placed to persuade their respective governments to alter their procedures in the light of their experiences in the recipient countries as long as it is agreed that such changes would result in aid effectiveness, perceived in terms of both cost and sustainability considerations.

The coordination pattern found here is not centralised and not formal. It is decentralised in the sense that the coordination takes place between groups of donors, rather than the whole donor community. Groups of donors with a common interest, for instance those working in the same sector, meet on a more regular basis to discuss policy and activities. These contacts are undertaken in an informal way. Sometimes in the form of committees, which are formed for some very specific purpose, sometimes simply by way of personal communication and contacts.

THE AID RELATIONSHIP AND THE PROSPECTS FOR COORDINATION

A number of conclusions can be drawn from the preceding analysis. Firstly, there have been initiatives towards establishing national structures for aid negotiations, management and utilisation. A number of donors, particularly UNDP and the World Bank, have moved in since the mid-1980s to support NCDP institutional capacity strengthening in the area of aid coordination. At the sectoral level, efforts are also currently ongoing in certain areas towards improved coordination and harmonisation of external resource utilisation. The Planning Unit at the Ministry of Education, for example, is receiving priority attention particularly from SIDA since this is the wing that is mandated to coordinate donor resources for the sector. Notwithstanding these initiatives, however, capacity and organisational weakness at both the national and sectoral levels still continues to make aid coordination a somewhat superficial and disjointed exercise. The absence of consultative mechanisms for all the aid coordinating agencies within the government system has, thus, continued to allow donor activities operate with considerable latitude outside the rather unclear government framework.

Secondly, aid monitoring and evaluation at the national level tends to assume a bilateral character whereby in the absence of a meaningful multilateral arrangement, each donor has continued to monitor and evaluate its own activities usually with some input from the government. Annual programme/project reviews are common. It is, nevertheless, not uncommon for a number of donors to independently monitor and evaluate their respective activities without government involvement. External 'experts' are normally brought into the country by donors for brief periods to evaluate the performance of externally-supported projects. While one cannot generalise about the utility value of such unilateral evaluation mechanisms, it can still be argued that analyses and reviews that are undertaken under tight time schedules and by evaluators that may not necessarily have the knowledge of the local conditions (even if they may possess better evaluation skills) could easily be of limited value.

As the 1986 UNDP report on the role of technical cooperation cautioned with respect to dependence on external experts:

> ... the professional background of foreign advisors is often predicated upon the existence of sophisticated support systems which are unavailable locally. People used to such an environment are often unable to re-think and simplify professional solutions. They tend to imitate structures ... which do not last—sometimes the project functions only whilst the expatriate is in post.[97]

A number of donor agencies have recognised the adverse effects of donor-dominated project and programme monitoring and evaluation mechanisms and have, thus, tried—and quite successfully in a number of cases—to involve the host government and local experts in such exercises. The adoption of well structured counterpart arrangements also tends to strengthen not only the notion of local ownership of donor supported projects but, more importantly, aid effectiveness and project sustainability.

---

[97] UNDP, 1986, p. 42.

Thirdly, the weaknesses in the processes of aid coordination under the current conditions in Zambia have resulted in the marginalisation of external resources when it comes to budgeting and planning. Although the periodic Consultative Group (CG) meetings in Paris between Zambia and its external resource providers do allow for a certain degree of meaningful dialogue on the setting of priority areas for aid intervention, it is equally noteworthy that such consultations and the timing of the disbursement of resources by donors are still not adequately synchronised. Not only is it difficult under such conditions to integrate external aid and national development planning and budgeting but, equally important, counterpart funds required to be sourced from the government's internally-generated revenue for the purpose of complementing external flows are usually non-existent or have to be obtained from extra-budgetary sources. Consequently, the effectiveness of donor-supported projects is often adversely affected.

Lastly, aid coordination in Zambia has generally been affected by how this process is defined and perceived by both the recipient government and, quite often, by the donors themselves. The notion of 'aid' or 'donor' coordination has an in-built anomaly that has far reaching consequences for aid effectiveness. It is hereby maintained that coordination should not be treated as 'donor' coordination if this process is to be meaningful and positive. Rather, it should be perceived as programme coordination. Under 'donor' coordination—which is the general perception currently prevailing in Zambia—the focus of attention has been on each donor and the nature and magnitude of its contribution to the recipient. Under such conceptualisation of coordination, the government acts more as a servicing organ that tries to understand and reconcile the various donors' activities and priorities at the planning, implementation, and monitoring levels. In this scenario, the priorities and procedures of the donors guide and dictate government policy. The consequences of this state of affairs are obvious: as long as (a) donors' preferences continue to assume an exalted status in the coordination process; (b) that they are allowed to 'run their own show'; (c) advise the government of what 'their' programmes are; (d) adopt operational and reporting procedures that are at variance and uncoordinated with the government's systems of operation; and (e) demand that their resources should be used exclusively for the projects that their governments, taxpayers and parliaments approve (even if this conflicts with recipient government priorities), then it is common knowledge that any effort towards improved coordination would be a difficult, if not redundant, exercise.

What is the preferred coordination seen from the perspective of Zambian interest? If coordination is seen as programme coordination rather than donor coordination, the point of departure should necessarily be the recipient government's priorities, procedures and plans. Under this preferred scenario, the standard format for aid negotiations, reception, utilisation and coordination should be designed for and/or by the government in ways that recognise the preferred and priority needs of the recipient. Where institutional and human resource weaknesses to rationally do this are observable (as is generally the case in Zambia), the role of the donors should be to assist in building the needed government capacities rather than attempting to supplant or substitute the recipient's *modus operandi* with what obtains in the donor's country.

Under programme coordination, the focus of the various actors' efforts is not on the individual donor's priorities or preferences but on the sectoral or programme priorities as defined by the government with or without the assistance of the donors. Under this scenario, the planning and implementation of the programmes lie exclusively in the recipient's hands. It is the general conclusion of this report that although the donor-driven, implemented and monitored project approach may be more efficient in the short term, it is strongly felt that the questions of ownership and sustainability are better realised under programme coordination that puts up front the priorities, mechanisms and processes of the recipient government. The former scenario may, of course, succeed in creating 'islands of efficiency' in aid management but such conditions can never be sustainable in the long term. Indeed, this phenomenon largely explains the frequency with which a number of aid-supported projects cease to exist immediately upon or shortly after the departure or significant reduction in donor resources, including technical assistance. What is the likelihood of achieving any changes in the present mode of aid coordination? Initially we listed a number of obstacles to coordination. What is needed to overcome them and can it be realistically achieved?

The first obstacle—lack of common visions and ideas—refers directly to the quality of the aid relationship as an arena for communication, or to paraphrase Long—a battlefield for knowledge. Although it might be difficult to achieve a common set of values, there is the need for an arena where different perceptions of aid and development are brought up and discussed. The present nature of the aid relationship in Zambia is a far cry from this desired state of affairs.

The second obstacle—lack of information—is also related to the quality of the aid relationship. Information has to be available and shared among the parties. It has to be distributed between the different interfaces of the whole aid arena. Today, information about what aid does and accomplishes is not available to everybody. Furthermore, the nature of the "aid relationship" as it presently exists means that establishing what is interesting and relevant information is determined largely by one of the parties—the donor agency. The pursuit of knowledge normally does not involve the ultimate beneficiaries of aid.

The third obstacle—donors having their own administrative procedures—becomes an issue in countries like Zambia where aid dependency is firmly established. A multitude of donors are involved in every key sector. Asking them to coordinate/harmonise their procedures with existing government administrative systems becomes difficult. Firstly, because the systems and procedures of donors are part of their governments' administrative systems. Secondly, because harmonisation requires clear host government procedures and a strong ability to enforce such coordination.

The fourth obstacle—the existence of hidden objectives—raises the question if there is anybody really interested in coordination? The fact that coordination does nor really take place may suggest that it is because none of the major stakeholders have any particular interest in it. In addition to the official objectives of aid, donors may have to consider pressures from their home constituencies for example commercial considerations leading to tied aid. Likewise, in the host country there are many actors who have their own reason for not wanting any coordination.

The fifth obstacle—the desire for "flagwaving"—concerns one of our most basic human needs: to tell the world that we are doing something very good. Coordination may infringe on this possibility, but not necessarily. It is possible to coordinate without losing our own profile. Furthermore, coordination may also improve the chances of projects succeeding and hence opportunities for "flagwaving". Finally, as coordination in itself carries a positive connotation it is possible that the mere fact that we engage in it opens up for "flagwaving".

The sixth obstacle—lack of transparency and accountability—is much more serious and difficult to rectify. It is close to the heart of the nature of the aid relationship. Our case studies provides some lessons learned, although we cannot on the basis of our material go into any details. Both parties in the aid relationship—the host government and the donor agency—are fairly well-regulated bureaucracies, with rules and procedures. The fact that the basis for accountability and transparency exists is, however, not important. It is rather the extent to which it is applied and enforced which needs to be discussed. Formally the aid relationship is regulated in the form of an agreement—a contract. It seems, however, that the function of a contract is not taken seriously. It is rarely used as an instrument for monitoring the relations between the parties. Agreements are not taken seriously and there are no institutional mechanisms for enforcement/sanctions. One example to illustrate the point. In the case studies of ZEMP and the JICA supported water project it appeared that the government had agreed to a division of labour which required it to supply manpower and other resources for carrying out the tasks it had agreed to perform within the project. The government failed to do so to the extent required, but nothing happened, the terms of the contract were never enforced by the other party. This then opens up for "informal" behaviour of bargaining, discussion or withdrawal from discussion of the critical issues. Attempts to rectify the problem caused by one party's inability to fulfil its part of the contract then lead to actions which will lack transparency and accountability.

It would seem from the above that achieving effective aid coordination is not primarily a technical matter. It is much more a function of the nature and quality of the aid relationship. The aid relationship needs to be changed before it will be possible to implement "real" coordination . The changes required and what determines the possibilities to effect such changes will be the subject of the next chapter, where we shall try to pull the various threads together into a comprehensive analysis of the aid relationship in Zambia.

Chapter 10

The Future of the Aid Relationship in Zambia—A Concluding Analysis

RETURNING TO THE PURPOSE

It is now time to pull the various threads together and make an attempt towards a conclusion. In this chapter we start by summarising our analytical approach. Then we proceed with a resume of the results from the case studies. The focus is on the type of interaction that takes place, at different points in time, between the Government of Zambia and the donors, and the type of conflicts that arise. Describing conflict patterns does not, however, take us very far towards understanding the main issue of this study: the aid relationship—its nature and quality—and the impact it has on aid effectiveness. This will require that we also try to identify the main factors causing the observed conflict patterns. The identification of these factors forms the point of departure for a discussion of how, and if, the aid relationship in its present shape can be reformed.

Our basic assumption has been that one could expect a strong causational link between the aid relationship and aid effectiveness. The basis for this assumption was outlined in some detail in Chapter 2. Aid, and aid evaluation, has for a long time been based on an understanding of knowledge which implies that there is a world out there which can be discovered. It is just a matter of finding the right facts, by applying the right scientific methods. This is an approach which hides a rather mechanistic approach to knowledge: how it is generated, distributed and used. For us, aid is rather more of a socially constructed and negotiated process. Reality is a social construction and the aid relationship is an arena for communication of such constructions. In the aid relationship the different actors, or stakeholders, should engage to exchange their various interpretations of the environment in which they work—a process for generating, distributing and sharing knowledge on aid effectiveness.

This knowledge has to be fed back into practice in order to improve aid effectiveness. In practical terms this would suggest project planning which, rather than providing a blueprint for action, facilitates continuous learning and interaction, procedures which allow the parties to readjust and modify programmes and projects as more is learned about the conditions with which they are trying to cope.[98] A well-functioning aid relationship should provide a basis for this to happen.

In the development debate a number of issues seem to surface time after time as major explanations as to why aid does not work as effectively as it should. First, the recipient has often been marginally involved in the early planning and design of a project. Donor priorities have tended to dominate and they have furthermore been erratic and inconsistent with recipient priorities. Second, recipient national institutions are inadequate to perform the tasks they are expected to perform due to political, administrative and human resource limitations. Third, aid has been poorly designed and sustainability considerations have not been sufficiently addressed by either donor or recipient. Fourth, aid has consistently stepped up the conditionalities attached to aid, which has given much less room for dialogue and thereby reduced the effectiveness of aid. Fifth, the mix of forms of aid in a given recipient country tends to be donor driven and sub-optimal. Sixth, aid coordination has not been sought by either donors or recipients, and its absence has limited the effectiveness of aid. Finally, the lack of transparency and accountability among donors and recipients undermines the effectiveness of aid.

What emerges out of these issues is the primacy attached to the organisations involved in delivering and receiving aid. There is no lack of evidence, nor awareness, of the importance of institutions for aid effectiveness. Efficient organisations operating within an appropriate institutional framework are one of the key pre-conditions for sustainable and effective aid. Aid evaluations frequently point this out as a major determinant of success or failure of aid. The organisations and structures in the host country are not strong enough to accommodate the resources that are provided through aid. The response from the aid community has also been forthcoming. There has been a shift in their programmes towards a stronger emphasis on institution-building and capacity development. Strengthening the capacity to receive is a key component in the strategy to improve aid effectiveness.

Within the context of aid, organisations cannot be analysed in isolation from each other. Aid is a joint venture where the parties are supposed to do something together. The way a donor and a host government organise their work constitutes the basis for the aid relationship. No matter how effective your own organisation is, if this is not matched by the other party's capacity. Inter-organisational cooperation is therefore a delicate balancing act. The effectiveness of the cooperation, in producing a maximum output, is determined by how well the parties can handle their differences and develop a working relationship which is more or less satisfactory to both parties. Thus, the interface of organisational cooperation is much more than the sum of its parts.

---

[98] Korten, D & F. Alfonso, 1981; and Rondinelli, D.A., 1990.

The peculiarity of the aid relationship, which distinguishes it from other organisational interfaces is its inequality and consequently tendencies towards dominance and conflict. This interaction, it was argued, can therefore not be limited to a study of the efficiency of formal structures for appraisal, monitoring and evaluation. We need another framework to be able to capture the dynamics of the aid relationship.

The aid relationship is a highly political relationship where outcomes are determined by power, authority and legitimation available to each of the principal actors involved. Since there are great differences in the various actors' possession of resources, power will be equally unevenly distributed. This will undoubtedly have an impact on the interaction which takes place in the aid relationship. Political games and conflicts can be expected to be a key feature. The ability of the aid relationship to manage conflicts is therefore crucial to a well-functioning aid relationship and hence aid effectiveness. There are two major factors contributing to this pattern of interaction. First, the unequal access to resources—financial and human—which is the fundamental rationale for aid. Second, the influence of the interest of various stakeholders. Aid is as much dominated by commercial and foreign policy motives, in addition to its "aid" objectives. There are strong interest groups, particularly on the donor side, with their own interest to protect and who can sometimes exercise a considerable leverage on decision-making.

This means that the aid relationship's normal state of affairs is dysfunctional. There is an in-built tendency towards marginalising one of the parties in the relationship. In a way one could say that it is this dysfunctionality which has been the subject matter of this study. A relationship which contains inequality, marginalisation etc. implies a high likelihood for conflicts. A reasonable analytical approach would then be to apply a conflict perspective on the aid relationship. What does this mean? The first point to be made is that there is no such thing as harmony. Any relationship between individuals and organisations is always filled with conflicts. There can be different kinds of conflicts, some are productive while others are quite unproductive. Harmony occurs when conflicts are handled in an effective way. The fact that everything seems peaceful should not be interpreted as the outcome of perfectly joint interests. It is rather the outcome of successful conflict management. We have taken our departure from a typology of conflict patterns in order to enable us to describe the conflicts that occur. Describing the nature of conflicts is the first step in providing a strategy for reforming the aid relationship.

Let us then turn to an examination of our findings. We shall start with the aid relationship as it emerged from the case studies.

THE AID RELATIONSHIP IN THE CASE STUDIES

This study has revealed some of Zambia's experiences with aid relationships and aid management at the micro as well as the macro level. Our case studies showed, often in a dramatic way, that at the micro level there are considerable costs to the recipient country from weak institutional structures and capacities. Donor behaviour at this level also demonstrated not only the diversity in their procedures and preferences but, perhaps more importantly, how such preferences have either perpetuated dependence relationships or contributed to more meaningful, sustainable and, hence, productive donor–recipient interactions. The analysis that follows, thus, attempts to draw general conclusions from Zambia's experience with aid on the basis of the study's four case studies.

We defined several types of conflict patterns—bargaining, problem solving, escalation, withdrawal and suppression—some more desirable than others. It was proposed that the first two were the most desirable in terms of a well-functioning interface.[99] The prevailing conflict patterns in the case studies were analysed. Conflict patterns are not, however, static. They change over time. In order to capture the dynamics of the relationship we have therefore tried to show the relationships as they evolved during the different stages of the project cycle. The results from the case studies are summarised in Figure 10.1.

Figure 10.1. *Actors and relationships in a JICA supported water programme*

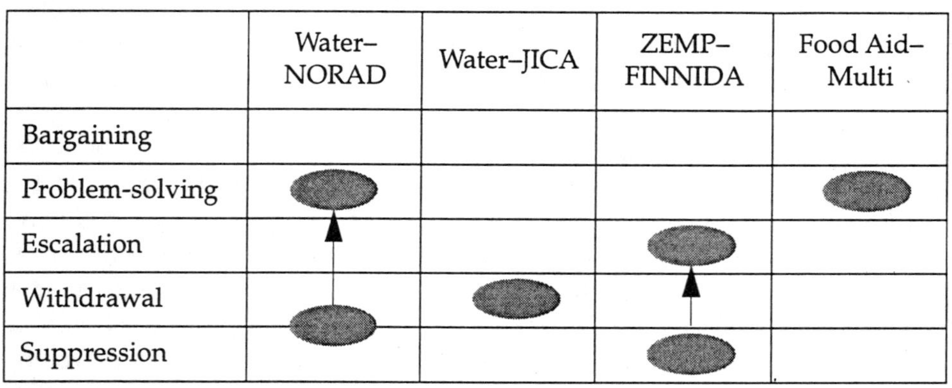

The case studies show that it is primarily when a problem is being identified and discussed that the parties engage in a frank and open discussion with each other. Productive conflict patterns of bargaining and problem solving characterise all case studies except one. In the Norwegian supported water

[99] The reader is advised to return to Chapter 2 for a more detailed discussion of each conflict type.

programme, the Government appear to have withdrawn from participation at the time when NORAD began assessing the possibility of developing a water and sanitation programme in Western Province.

The case studies would also suggest that when the actual project design is being considered, the Government tend to withdraw from engaging in a dialogue with the donor. The donor is largely left to organise things as he finds appropriate. The exception here is the 1993 drought relief programme, where the government showed a very strong commitment through all phases of the intervention. The tendency towards non-productive conflict patterns continues in two of the cases—the Finnish/Swedish schoolbook project and the Japanese water project. What is interesting to see, however, is the shift that takes place in the Norwegian project. Half-way through implementation the conflict pattern changes, largely a response to reports on low effectiveness, and a pattern of problem solving gradually replaces the previous pattern of a non-dialogue.

The pattern that emerges in the case studies suggests that when the conflict pattern in the aid relationship is characterised by "withdrawal" or "suppression", it contributes to the perpetuation of a number of donors opting to operate with considerable and uninterrupted freedom outside the government system. The government either "withdrew" from direct involvement and confrontation, or "suppressed" its discontent regarding how things were evolving. In other words, a pattern leading towards marginalisation of the government in the development effort.

Two of the case studies in particular seem to represent the extreme ends of this dichotomy and do illustrate the gains to be derived from engaging in active conflict management and resolution. The first one is the NORAD-supported Water Supply and Sanitation Programme in Western Province (Chapter 6). As demonstrated, the programme started as a largely donor-driven initiative with NORAD operating outside the government framework. Considerable discontent was registered by the local level Department of Water Affairs (DWA) regarding how the programme was bei...
mented particularly since it create...
government with no coordination at
sioned evaluation through which the
expressed their concerns, the donor a
positive steps in 1985 particularly at
organisational structure and manage
programme onwards has been an outs
ness to sustainability considerations. N
sources channelled through the recipi
the lower level, including grassroots,
volved, especially through the CEP con
and monitoring. Community participat
lised. Equally significant, this programm

ties have been fully integrated into the recipient government system through the WASHE concept that has adopted decentralised delivery mechanisms. There are at present no NORAD technical assistance personnel two to three years before the programme is phased out. Although this study identified a number of programme weaknesses that tend to compromise the level of its sustainability upon the withdrawal of NORAD funds, most of such constraints relate to the weak central government preparedness and its failure to take advantage of the opportunities being provided by the programme's phasing out modalities.

At the other extreme of the continuum, the FINNIDA/SIDA-supported Zambia Educational Materials Project (see Chapter 5), represents a good example of a project where not only is the government unprepared to acknowledge openly its expressed dissatisfaction with how the project was implemented (and, therefore, continues to adopt suppression-cum-withdrawal modes in its interaction with FINNIDA) but, equally important, the donor has not demonstrated willingness to accommodate criticisms levelled against it by independent evaluation teams. The 1991 findings of the project's Phase II evaluation team (consisting of external consultants and a locally-based and respected professor of education) came out with very critical revelations about the organisational, management style, and structural weakness of ZEMP. The project's isolation from the government system was particularly challenged. Rather than taking advantage of the criticisms, FINNIDA's locally-based personnel challenged the evaluation team's findings and offered to the government their defence in support of their modus operandi. The consequence of the above development has been predictable. FINNIDA continued to operate "as usual" and few organisational changes were effected. With the departure of the long standing Project Coordinator, a replacement was effected. Efforts to integrate the project into the government system have since been made. However, the FINNIDA project support to ZEMP was scheduled to be phased out in 1994 and the project's sustainability upon the departure of FINNIDA personnel and other resources is not readily predictable.

The Drought Emergency In Southern Africa (DESA) offers a striking contrast to the other cases in several ways. First of all, there was the close coordination between donors, bilateral as well as multilateral, and the [illegible]mbian authorities in terms of problem identification and the design of the [illegible]l relief operation. Joint problem solving and bargaining were the [illegible]nt conflict modes during the whole DESA operation. Secondly, the [illegible] the operation deliberately involved the community level for [illegible] needs and food distribution. Thirdly, the organisational struc[illegible] established for the relief operation were kept after it was [illegible]ew mandates. This basically meant two things. Firstly, in[illegible]an preparedness for limiting the impact of future [illegible]stablishment a permanent vulnerability monitoring system. Secondly, an increased capacity for post-recovery developmental activities.

What conclusions can we then draw from these emerging conflict patterns in the aid relationship?

At a more general level, when the interface between the recipient and donor organisations is characterised in organisational conflict terms, one conclusion that could be derived from the four case studies covered in this study is that the typical donor-aided project has received limited guidance from the government at almost all the levels of its circle. For reasons not *always* readily apparent, the government has generally tended to place considerable faith in the donor, especially when it is a bilateral donor agency, in the definition of what is required and how best it could be attained. Evidence, albeit limited, suggests that because of weak institutional structures; low analytical capacity; and unclarity of policy in some cases, the government has often found it difficult to "voice" its concern to the donors even in cases where it believes things should be done differently. Consequently, as Figure 10.1 shows, when one perceives aid relationships in conflict-resolving terms, the Zambian government has often either "suppressed" its dissatisfaction with how the donor conducts its business or has tended to "withdraw" from rocking the boat, as it were, in order to create an atmosphere of harmony with its cherished donors. Conflict avoidance on the part of the government has, thus, tended to characterise the donor–recipient relational/conflictual interface in Zambia.

The above tendencies have contributed to the perpetuation of a number of donors opting to operate with considerable and uninterrupted freedom outside the government system. With the exception of the food aid case study, all bilateral donors have tended to gravitate towards "undesirable" modes in the sense that they have operated with minimum interference from the government. The government has more often than not, been marginalised at the project design, implementation, monitoring and evaluation stages.

Thus, withdrawal or suppression seem to be the dominant mode of conflict in Zambia's aid relationship.

Perhaps the most important lesson is that conflict avoidance in the donor–recipient interactive interface is not necessarily rational under certain circumstances. Due to Zambia's characteristic obsession with "peace" and "good relations" in its international relations, the perception that harmony is always a good thing and conflict a bad thing seems to feature in the country's relationships with its donors. Moderation to this norm is often a product, not of the recipient, but of the donor itself. And yet conflict per se should not always be perceived to be a bad thing in aid relationships. By trying hard to make things appear "normal", even when deep rooted dissatisfaction with the project cycle's modus operandi is evident, an atmosphere of false harmony sets in.

One serious consequence of the above relational pattern in donor–recipient interaction is that both parties miss the opportunity to confront challenges that must be faced, appraised and resolved to their mutual interest vis-à-vis the common goal of making aid effective. In organisational theory, we are reminded that it is precisely the rational articulation of the organisations' problems and areas of conflict that facilitates the basis for conflict resolution and improved performance. By attempting to suppress areas of disagreement, on the other hand, individuals and organisations miss the opportunity to productively take corrective actions.

EXPLAINING THE NATURE OF THE AID RELATIONSHIP

A number of deficiencies regarding the relationship between Zambia and its donors were revealed. The dominant mode of local participation, at different stages in the project cycle, was characterised by withdrawal from, or suppression of conflict, and this did not bode well for the effectiveness of aid. How do we then explain these patterns?

The question is important since its answer is the starting point for developing a strategy for more productive relationships. There is, of course, not one answer to the question, but several. Principally the answers can be sought in two places: inside the organisations that participate in the interface and in the immediate and external context of the interface.

We will start by looking at the intra-organisational factors that can explain the prevailing mode of interaction in the interface. In order to explain why an organisation acts the way it does it is useful to look at the reward system, or incentive structure, that dominates the organisation. Admittedly, to pursue such a discussion here requires much more in-depth analysis of the participating organisations than what we have been able to do. Still, however, there are some interesting features emerging out of the case studies.[100] Let us start by looking at how the availability of resources determines organisational behaviour at the interface.

AVAILABILITY OF RESOURCES

In Zambia the general deprived state of the economy is a prime factor explaining Zambian participation in the aid relationship. In practice the Zambian government administration does not work they way it was intended. Its basic structure has remained largely unchanged since independence.

---

[100] It should be pointed out to the reader that our analysis of organisational behaviour is very general. We do not differentiate between, for instance, the various Zambian organisations that participate in an aid intervention. Neither do we distinguish between different donor agencies. This approach is deliberate for two reasons. First, we do not possess enough evidence on the functioning of each type of organisation. Second, there are some analytical advantages to be gained from not going into too many details.

At that time it was more or less able to perform its activities but since then a lot of things have changed, making it more and more inefficient. The system as it functions today is highly centralised, marginalising all levels below the central. Furthermore, the demands on the system in terms of planning and implementation are now so great that it cannot cope.

The fact that Zambia generally lacks resources for undertaking anything on its own and also effectively maintaining its organisation with which it participates in aid projects creates an incentive structure which works against any attempt to engage in a constructive dialogue. There is hardly any possibility for the GOZ to mobilise the resources needed for its participation in all stages of a project cycle. Few organisational units in the government administration have sufficient resources. This opens up for various types of behaviour incompatible with a good aid relationship. Staff need to supplement their meagre salaries in various ways. They lack transport etc. to perform their jobs. Their incentive to participate as active counterparts is therefore limited. Too often they may choose to abstain from any productive critique of a project simply to ensure that their benefits are not threatened. Consequently, a passive partner is the result who is all too happy to see the donor run the show.

This kind of behaviour within a Zambian organisation can be understood. But what is more difficult to comprehend is the fact that donors play along. Time after time we can see projects designed as if the GOZ was a capable partner. The best example is perhaps ZEMP, another is the JICA water project. Each time the results are the same—projects slowly withering away after the donor has withdrawn. It seems to be that donors presume the existence of a capacity and motivation which are not there. For those who have followed the aid debate over the last 10 years, this conclusion may appear trivial. A number of aid evaluations have pointed to these weaknesses in project designs. The interesting thing, however, is that this "common knowledge" has not led to any changes in donor behaviour. The situation continue to persist. This apparent neglect of taking into consideration Zambia's capacity to absorb aid when planning the quantity and quality of aid can not be explained by mismanagement or incompetence within the aid agencies. The true reasons are much more fundamental to the mode of operation of international aid. First of all, in most donor countries the amount of the state budget allocated to aid is predetermined in terms of a percentage of, for example, the GDP. Within the international donor community, especially the DAC of the OECD, there has been a strong pressure on donor countries to meet the 1% target. This situation where the amount to be spent is pre-determined, introduces an immediate pressure on the donor agencies to disburse the money. Some donors also use a system of country frames, where budget allocations are pre-determined over a longer period of time. In the case of Swedish aid to Guinea-Bissau, this had led to more or less automatic increases in support every year.[101]

Thus, there are systemic forces creating an urge to move money. This immediately affects the incentive structure in the agency. Programme officers can look forward to good career prospects if they push money. They are less likely to be punished in career terms if the project fares badly. Theoretically, there are counter-balances to prevent this happening in the form of elaborate appraisal procedures. Still, there is evidence to show that these systems lend themselves too easily to manipulation. As Mosley, Harrigan and Toye point out with respect to the practice of the World Bank, "a lot of massaging of proposals goes on to ensure momentary acceptability by such means as excessively optimistic primary product price forecasts".[102]

The difficulties this creates in terms of aid effectiveness become very visible in a country like Zambia, where the capacity to receive fast moving money is very limited. Donors are forced to bypass the government, establish parallel structures etc. But this can soon turn out to be a temporary panacea. This was experienced by Sweden when it demanded a large Zambian involvement in the aid programme in terms of manpower and finance. The Zambian government obviously had other priorities. As a result of this conflict of interest most projects and programmes were initiated and, in practice also implemented, by Sweden. Eventually all the three major Swedish sector programmes faced disbursement problems.[103]

Actions such as these run a high risk of marginalising the Zambian authorities to the point of no involvement and commitment, and thereby creating an unproductive aid relationship.[104]

AID MANAGEMENT CAPACITY

In the current debate on aid effectiveness it has often been pointed out that aid is strongly supply driven. Specific donor interests dominate decisions on what should be done and why. To a large extent this is also true of the aid relationship in Zambia. But there are other stakeholders, apart from the donor agency itself, who have specific interests in aid. One important group are consultants/technical experts. Most donor agencies use consultants for running the projects. This occurred in all our case studies, except the DESA where local NGOs were the dominant implementing organisations.

101 Svedberg, P., A. Olofsgård & B. Ekman, 1994, p. 137.

102 Mosley, P., J. Harrigan & J. Toye, 1991, p. 48.

103 Bigsten, A. et al., 1994, p. 46.

104 "Usually the career incentives in any donor agency are to move money swiftly and at a low administrative cost; banks want to lend, and aid agencies want to use the money voted to them by governments—otherwise these funds may be lost to the agency at the end of a fiscal period ..." (Lipton, M & J. Toye, 1991, p. 170.)

Needless to say they may have strong incentives in continuation of the projects and are also in a position where they can influence decisions to prolong a project, or change its course etc.

However, it is not uncommon that these interests converge with interests on the host country side, which makes it very difficult to critically assess a project and its effectiveness.[105] In a project there is an operating core consisting of foreign experts and their local counterparts. Both stand to benefit from participating in the project. If the distribution of benefits is acceptable to both parties, in such a way that both stand to gain from a continuation of the project (in one form or another), it is obvious that they can form quite an influential force in the decision-making process.

Linked to the issue of stakeholder interests is another doubtful donor assumption: that the different units in the government administration actually represent the ultimate beneficiaries of aid. It is apparent from our cases that the decision-making process in an aid project rarely involves the ultimate beneficiaries of aid. This is a reflection of one of the basic principles of aid. It is assumed that the host government represents the interests of the people, in one way or another. The history of aid makes this a doubtful assumption. In many cases one could expect the state, and its various units, to have interests which are different from the target group of aid. The basic mode of operation of aid actually acts as a barrier to an effective dialogue with the target group. This means that voices of concern never enter into the interface, important knowledge is foregone and the chances of unproductive conflict patterns occurring are strengthened.

Firstly, one of the most important pre-requisites for effective aid management is a functional as well as a carefully thought-out national institutional framework within which external resources are mobilised, acquired, utilised, monitored and evaluated in a way that recognises the recipients' priorities (be they defined as the whole country itself or the actual target community/group within the country). And yet in the Zambian case, institutional weaknesses at both the national and sectoral levels have been uncovered in this study that have contributed significantly to aid ineffectiveness.

The government system of Zambia was built after independence largely along the lines of the previous colonial administration. This was a system designed for the purpose of control, rather than development. As such it is a highly centralised system. It is composed of four levels. The central level of the line ministries, the provincial level, the district level and the village level. It was set up to facilitate a flow of information from the bottom to the top, providing basic information from the village level to the responsible line ministry. But the final decision was always taken at the central level. The political system of Zambia—the one-party state—further amplified the cen-

105 Berg, E., 1993, pp. 133–135.

tralised tradition of the colonial administration. Already during the first republic, the system gravitated towards a strong presidential power. Kaunda virtually made all decisions himself, not necessarily involving the cabinet or the civil service. By the time of the second republic economic decision-making was totally centralised. The president had by then abandoned collective decision-making and relied on a small group of advisors.[106]

The decision-making process contained in this system implies a conflict with the administrative requirements of aid programmes, although not necessarily with the donors' own administrative procedures. Aid aiming for the social sectors often requires an involvement of the grassroots. Zambia's centralised decision-making has clear difficulties in accommodating these requirements.

This is a conflict with serious consequences for the effectiveness of aid:

> The problem is rather delicate, since sustainability of projects beyond external assistance depends on administrative commitment. If successful implementation demands that the centralised decision-making system be by-passed by donors, then the sustainability of projects is also called in question. Attempts to by-pass the administration have also faced another problem: The centralised system results in poor manpower capacity at district level and below.[107]

Moreover, the existence of a multiplicity of donor procedures, demands and conditionalities has tended to generate a functional strain on the already ill-equipped and overstretched government bureaucracy whose absorptive capacity is evidently weak. This highlights the need for coordination. Not only to avoid duplication of efforts, but also to make more efficient use of scarce government resources.

At present, despite the existence of institutions and mechanisms that are supposed to provide the forum for improved aid management and coordination at the national and sectoral levels, such arrangements are not performing adequately. One example can illustrate the point: although NCDP is in charge of aid coordination and monitoring at the macro level, this study discovered that the actual practice shows that it is the Ministry of Finance and the central bank that are actually in charge of debt management as well as the negotiation of loans and grants. While, traditionally, there is nothing abnormal about such an arrangement, it is the absence of meaningful collaboration (both formal and informal) between these arms of government that has resulted in aid management in Zambia remaining a highly disjointed and uncoordinated exercise. Equally revealing has been the discovery in this study that all the aid coordinating institutions at the macro level suffer from serious structural and human capacity limitations that include weak organisational systems; inadequate and unreliable policy-cum-planning databases; the absence of well-trained, remunerated, motivated and experienced per-

---

106 Andersson, P. & M. Ndulo, 1992; and Gulhati, R., 1989.

107 Bigsten, A, et al., 1994, p. 47.

sonnel; and poor financial management and accounting systems that have tended to threaten accountability. The analytical capacity of most of the aid management institutions in the country is generally limited to the collection of basic data on aid flows with very little effort towards policy-relevant analyses that would allow the government to possess the competence needed to meaningfully bargain with, and guide donors towards well articulated policies and priorities.

Zambia's ability to fulfil its part of the development project is therefore severely reduced, at all levels, which means that donors are forced to take on functions which they are not really supposed to, and sometimes even ill-equipped for, in order to ensure aid delivery. Donors are encouraged to either include 'gate-keeping' functions in their interaction with the recipient and/or simply go around the government system altogether by creating parallel project management and implementation systems.

Apart from the necessity for intra-government coordination vis-à-vis external resources management, this study has also highlighted the importance of realistic coordination between donors and recipients to assure aid effectiveness. Donor–recipient coordination is important to the extent that it facilitates the national systems having more informed picture of the nature and extent of external support and using such knowledge to strengthen both its definition and redefinition of external involvement as well as to consolidate its aid management capacity through an in-depth knowledge of what the donor is doing. By close monitoring through, for instance, consultative meetings with donors, the government's seriousness of purpose would be revealed, itself an important catalyst for increased external support.

Equally critical in the analysis is the importance placed on coordination among and within the main players in the donor–recipient interface so that their collective actions are harmonised in a way that avoids undesirable duplication of effort that tends to complicate both the government's and the donor's aid management function.

Although donor–government coordination usually receives most of the attention, this study has particularly pointed to the lack of coordination among government institutions as being equally important. Serious institutional weaknesses at both the national, provincial and district levels, explain the deficiencies in the government framework within which aid is expected to be mobilised, received, utilised, monitored and evaluated. Although there exist institutions and mechanisms that are expected to provide the forum for intra-government coordination at these levels, they are currently not performing according to expectations.

CONDITIONALITY

We have already hinted at possible influences from the external context on the nature of the aid relationship. The most important of these are probably related to the issue of conditionality. For various reasons, frustration with aid effectiveness being one, economic recession in the donor countries another, donors have over the last 10–15 years stepped up conditionalities.

The concept of conditionality must, however, be qualified. At the lowest level we may find conditionality in terms of accountability and transparency. How have funds been used and accounted for? Policy conditionalities, usually requiring certain economic policies to be in place as a condition for continued aid are the next step. The ultimate level is political conditionality. Aid is then conditioned by the extent to which the host government is prepared to respect human rights and introduce democracy, normally in the form of a multiparty system.[108]

The higher the level of conditionality the more complications are introduced into the aid relationship. It is noteworthy that donors have preferred to concentrate their conditionalities on the higher levels, rather than enforcing conditionality in terms of accountability. Donor frustrations with Zambia and its lacklustre performance have led them to take an ever larger responsibility for the country to the point of formulating its policies in important areas. Political conditionality further strengthens the unequal nature of the aid relationship since it interferes with what are actually basic sovereignty issues. A particular feature of conditionality, which makes it hard to digest, is its negative bias: cuts, reductions, closures, dismantling etc. The effectiveness of the aid relationship would probably be higher if conditionalities were associated with something positive: increasing growth, public health, better schools etc. Instead of assuming that the supply response will come automatically as soon as all the "negative" things have been done.[109]

This impact is further strengthened by the lack of coordination of conditionality. Sometimes one could get the impression that donors to Zambia in terms of policies form a united front. The picture of bilateral donors lining up behind the World Bank and the IMF is only partially true. There are differences, in terms of nature of conditionalities, which make harmonisation difficult. Conditionalities can be more or less precise in terms of performance indicators. They can be quantitative as well as qualitative, hence more or less easy to measure. Furthermore, the actual number of conditions introduces the problem of weighing. Zambia may succeed in meeting two or three of the targets, but fail miserably in other indicators. How shall we weigh the value of success and failure? Needless to say, it is not possible by rather subjective views from each of the parties. The question is to what ex-

108 One of the most ardent critics of the World Bank and the IMF, describes the process of policy formulation in the following way: "The process is rather one in which the international agencies attempt to ensure that policies on which they themselves have decided are adopted by the governments hoping to receive aid." (Hayter, T., 1971, pp. 154–156.)

109 Engberg-Pedersen, P., 1996, p. 121.

tent one of the parties is the one who decides, or if there is some sort of bargaining taking place.

One might think that uncoordinated donors would open up a splendid opportunity for Zambia to "divide and rule" and thus compensate for its lack of power. This has not been the case, however, for two reasons. In the Paris Club meetings donors have normally managed to negotiate away their differences and presented Zambia with a united front. Although cross-conditionalities are not always explicit, informal cross-conditionalities seem to be effectively practised. Zambia, for its part, has not always been particularly good in presenting policy alternatives to the ruling policy paradigm of the donors.

A further complication arises if donor conditionalities vary to such an extent that compliance in one case means non-compliance in another—whatever one does is double jeopardy.

Accountability, on the other hand, provides openings for a good aid relationship, as it makes clear who is going to do what and what happens if the contract is not lived up to.

The most visible expression of Zambia's relationship to its donors can of course be seen in the magnitude of aid flows to the country over the years. At the level of aid volume, the Zambian experience has registered significant fluctuations in the past ten years or so. Violent movements in actual aid flows have been observed. To a large extent this can be explained by the country's macro economic policy changes and how these have pleased or offended the country's major bilateral and multilateral donors. As soon as the Zambian government U-turned on the economic liberalisation path following the introduction of the regime of controls in May 1987 when the country unilaterally abandoned the IMF and World Bank-supported programme, a proportionate reduction in external resource inflow was registered. In particular, the government's decision in 1985 to adopt a comprehensive Structural Adjustment Programme was greeted with considerable positive interest from many donors who supported the emerging liberalised economy in which private sector-led economic choices became superior to centrally-determined options. The volume of bilateral and multilateral aid flows showed, on average, a marked upward trend.

It is, nevertheless, noteworthy that some variations among donors' responses were observable. The return in November 1991 to the policy of economic liberalisation, particularly since this also embraced political liberalisation and a change to a government that promised to hasten the reform process, saw with it a U-turn by a number of donors who rededicated themselves to the support of the country. What the above picture suggests is that the aid flow pattern in Zambia has been significantly conditioned by the donors' faith (or lack of it) in the government's ability and commitment to design and implement a stable reform programme.

The increasing use of conditionalities has also been reflected in the composition of aid. Aid has been subjugated to SAP, in itself a masterpiece of conditionality. Balance of payments support has grown in importance as SAP has been securing a strong foothold. The reasons for this shift from project aid to programme aid are quite similar for most countries in Sub-Saharan Africa. When economic performance became an important determinant of aid flows in the 1970s and onwards, a wide range of performance criteria were introduced. Macroeconomic performance, the pricing environment, public policies in welfare and poverty areas, the performance of public institutions etc. These were normative criteria indeed, with a clear set of policies behind them. Aid then became a matter of rewarding those that met the criteria and punishing those who did not. The project mode of transferring aid then became inefficient. It is a slow, cumbersome way of giving aid. It cannot be made to respond quickly as was the case with programme aid. What was needed was an instrument which made it possible to enforce conditionalities. Programme aid was such an instrument.

Zambia's rollercoaster relationship with donors on policy issues is well known. The number of development plans which the country has formulated over the last 15–20 years may give the observer the impression that there is something wrong with Zambia's capacity to formulate strategies and policies. This would most likely be an incorrect assumption. What we have witnessed can be described as a conditionality game.[110]

This game can be divided into three stages. In the first stage there is a negotiating process leading up to an agreement (Or the parties simply decide to break away from each other). This agreement outlines in more or less detail, the agreed policy changes that are going to take place, and the relevant performance indicators. The second phase is implementation of the agreement. The host government now decides on how much of the agreement it can possibly honour. Sometimes the donors have to intervene at this stage and assist in the implementation process. The third phase, finally, is concerned with evaluation of compliance. To what extent has the host country lived up to the agreement. The outcome from these discussions determines whether a second round of financing will take place.

What are the motives for Zambia and its donors to enter into this game? Zambia has basically two motives for participation. First, it needs to maximise the inflow of aid. Second, it wants to acquire these resources at the lowest possible price (reducing conditionalities). The donor has slightly other motives. First, it wants to maintain a presence in the country and the disbursement levels. Second, it want to extract as much policy reform as it possibly can in order to ensure as much control as possible.

[110] The conditionality game is extensively discussed in Mosley, P., J. Harrigan & J. Toye (1991). We have adapted their argument to the Zambian circumstances.

These partly conflicting objectives set the conditions of the game. The donor can only enforce conditionalities up to the point where it becomes impossible to lend/give any money. Zambia, on the other hand, can only resist conditionalities up to the point where donors feel that it is generally useless to disburse any aid at all. The outcome of the game is determined by the respective strength each party brings to the bargaining table. The strength Zambia brings to the bargaining table is conditioned by two things: first, the state of the economy; second the struggle between those who stand to gain from a shift in policies (as contained in the SAP) and those who will lose out if such a shift takes place.

The losers from SAP related conditionalities were the winners from the economic system developed by the one-party state and the development strategy of Kaunda. Actors who gain from subsidised services and protected markets (cheap electricity, petrol and fuel for urban consumers, access to rationed forex, subsidised fertilisers and credits for "richer" farmers, employees of subsidised parastatal industries). Within the government one could expect different attitudes from the Central Bank and the Ministry of Finance. They are in charge of basic macroeconomic management, and in general have less of a problem to accept SAP related conditionalities than line ministries such as agriculture, health, commerce and industry etc. The latter will be the ones to experience first hand the short- to medium term consequences of adjustment.

Zambia's rocky relationship with primarily the World Bank and the IMF can be interpreted as the expression of these internal struggles. As the economy has been getting progressively worse, Zambia's bargaining situation has deteriorated. The "losers" from SAP lost their strength as they could not formulate a viable alternative strategy. Donors have been able to extract quite considerable conditionalities in exchange for their aid. Not only has the "old" economic regime been dismantled, so has the political system of the Kaunda days.

THE AID RELATIONSHIP AND AID EFFECTIVENESS

Notwithstanding the amount and pattern of external resource inflow to developing countries, there has been an increasing concern among both donors and recipients world-wide that the intended impact of external assistance has remained marginal even where actual volumes have increased significantly. This is in spite of a number of African countries taking on board most of the conditionalities specified by donors, including the now trendy non-economic ones such as those pertaining to democratic political systems; good governance; and environmental considerations.

Leaving aside the issue of establishing exactly how effective aid has been, our concern has been the causational links that exist between the aid relationship and aid effectiveness. In other words we are not trying to answer Cassen's old question: Does aid work in Zambia?

Initially we defined aid effectiveness according to two criteria: 1) The project's or programme's ability to achieve its set goals and objectives. 2) The degree to which such achievements are sustainable.

The extent to which objectives are reached cannot be interpreted in a mechanistic fashion—meeting some pre-defined performance target. It also involves the issue of whether the objectives are the right ones—is the project doing the right thing, in the right place and at the right cost. Determining what are the right objectives is a matter for the aid relationship. What is the "right" objective is a social construction. Only if the aid relationship allows all involved/concerned parties in a project to bring in their views on what the objectives should be will we approximate the "right" objectives.

The concept of sustainability is crucial for our definition of aid effectiveness. Not only shall the individual aid intervention meet its set objectives, but the benefits should be realised over an extended period that goes beyond the completion of the aid activity.

The aid relationship is important for sustainability since it requires the ability of both the donor and the recipient to clearly conceptualise and effectively implement a process of institutional capacity building and/or strengthening in a way that does the following:

- takes advantage of the most abundant indigenous resource, namely, manpower, and trains it to be able to handle project management, implementation and evaluation beyond external support;
- puts in place a realistic organisational framework within which project sustenance could be consolidated and guaranteed;
- ensures that the availability of physical, financial, and technological resources that are required for project success and effectiveness are assured during the life span of the project.

The above three considerations contain the fundamentals of sustainable aid. The extent to which these issues are properly addressed at the time of project appraisal, design and implementation, is linked to the effectiveness of the aid relationship.[111]

Sustainability is, however, a concept beset by methodological problems, which makes it difficult to evaluate whether an aid project is sustainable or not. The major difficulty has to do with time. First, the determination or measurement of sustainability requires a historical perspective. Quite some time may elapse from project completion to the time when it is appropriate to analyse sustainability. Second, what we understand as a sustainable project at one point in time, may have changed completely 10–15 years later.

[111] Wai, D., 1994.

Criteria for sustainability change with the times and depending on when we choose to measure them, we may come up with quite different results. These comments may seem very academic. In reality there are few aid projects which will lend themselves easily to an analysis of sustainability. One reason is because sustainability concerns are seldom seriously addressed during appraisal. Another reason is that nobody really cares to give sustainability an operational definition.

Thus, we are therefore not in a position to state whether or not any of the projects examined in the case studies are sustainable or not. However, it is unsatisfactory to leave the issue without an intelligent discussion of at least the prospects for sustainability. Our starting point is the previous three conditions for sustainable aid: human resource development, organisational efficiency and resources.

Let us start with the first condition—the importance of training and developing local human resources. To begin with, it could be concluded from all the case studies but one (the food aid case covered in Chapter 7) that considerations of project sustainability beyond donor support were never a priority issue when the projects started (i.e. at the stage of project conceptualisation and planning). And yet this is one of the most important pre-conditions of project effectiveness. The aspect of human resource development and how it has been handled in the four case studies is quite instructive. With respect to the FINNIDA-supported ZEMP, one observes that although the project did contribute to considerable knowledge acquisition by locals through its training programme, the concept of counterparts was superficially handled. In almost all the cases, indigenous personnel that were identified as counterparts to foreign "advisors" possessed very limited controlling power and authority. The advisory functions of the technical advisors, thus, fell short of equipping the local counterparts with the needed skills.

Similarly, the initial phase of the NORAD-supported Water Supply and Sanitation programme (Chapter 6) exhibited serious weaknesses with regard to the full integration of the indigenous human resources in the donor's programme of activities. The ultimate expression was the appointment of a Norwegian as Provincial Water Engineer. It was only after the donor accepted the critical recommendations eight years after the start of the project that corrective steps were taken. Likewise, the JICA-supported Groundwater Development Project in Southern Province (Chapter 8), while possessing the component on training local experts in Japan, overlooked the importance of an elaborate counterpart system. Perhaps the most significant weakness of the JICA-supported project at this level was its failure to build into its operational scheme the integration of community participatory mechanisms in the maintenance of the supplied water points.

Unlike the three case studies above, the 1992 donor support to the alleviation of drought impact involved, right from the beginning, the participation of national, regional and local level institutions and groups of people in the relief planning and management operations. Beyond the drought relief effort, the exercise recognised the importance of sustainability considerations by converting the principle of relief into recovery, the latter involving the building up of national and local level preparedness to cope with similar natural hardships in future.

Turning to the second major consideration of sustainability, namely, a realistic organisational framework, the four case studies reveal diverse experiences. At one level, the government's previously analysed weak structures for coordinating donor-supported programmes has compromised their effectiveness. This seemed to be the fate of the JICA programme, which really assumed the existence of something which was not there—enough organisational capacity from the Department of Water Affairs. At another level which is related to, or encouraged by, the first level, some donors have shown an inclination to prefer operating outside the state system. In the case of ZEMP, for example, project planning, management and financial decision-making were concentrated in the hands of the Helsinki-based consulting firm through its appointed Project Coordinator located in Lusaka. Consequently, the largely independent organisation and management structure of ZEMP succeeded in isolating the project from the Zambian government system. A very similar experience was found in the early stages of the NORAD water programme where a Norwegian consultancy firm effectively ran the programme.

One important consideration emerging from the style of project management exemplified by ZEMP, is noteworthy particularly under the current liberalised economic regime in Zambia where the private sector is being encouraged to assume the tasks previously dominated by the state sector. This is the caution to the effect that much as the use of a private company in implementing donor-assisted projects in the recipient country has its important merits, care ought to be taken at the project design and management structure levels so as to avoid the likelihood of commercial considerations, which are short-term, overshadowing the more long-term aspects of project sustainability. While private companies' commercial and profit considerations are usually important vis-à-vis their preferred implementation modalities, the recipient country's more strategic interests such as the engagement of local personnel and the subsequent transfer of knowledge to them could easily be overlooked if they are not specifically spelled out in the contract with the private implementing company.

Against the above realisation, it can be argued that while the foreign experts have quite efficiently performed their assigned task of facilitating the development, production and distribution of textbooks, it is the actual process through which such achievements were realised that is at issue when considerations of effectiveness come to the fore. In other words, efficiency should not always be seen as being synonymous with effectiveness. Thus, while efficiency can be defined as doing things right, effectiveness essentially entails doing the right things right. In this respect, it can be argued that without proper considerations at the project planning level, it is easy for the implementing firm to do very efficiently the wrong things. In this respect, it is both the donor and the recipient government that should shoulder the blame for not designing the contract with the private implementing firm in a way that best reconciles the company's commercial interests with the long-term project sustainability and effectiveness considerations.

Notwithstanding the above, it is worth noting that sustainability is also a function of the resources the parties can bring into the aid project. This is our third condition. Of particular importance is the government's capacity to mobilise the needed resources in terms of equipment and manpower. It is a sad fact that the Zambian administration, at all levels, is in a serious crisis, with a limited capacity to undertake its part of the development effort. In two of the case studies, ZEMP and the NORAD water project, we did a detailed study of the involvement of government structures at the provincial, district and village level. The results clearly suggest a substantial marginalisation. The aid relationships as such do not involve these bodies to any significant extent. This is particularly the case at the important, early phases of the project cycle. Joint discussions regarding problem identification and project design, to the extent that they take place, seem to be conducted solely at the level of the line ministry. Lower administrative levels are, at best, informed about a project and its purpose. The consequences of this lack of participation from those most concerned and affected by the aid intervention, were clearly demonstrated in both the Japanese water project and the Finnish/Swedish schoolbook project.

The case studies pointed out the importance of weak institutional capacity on the Zambian side as a major determinant of the aid relationship. Their inefficiency, and marginalisation appeared as a chief factor preventing an effective dialogue from taking place. The capacity of the recipient government to identify the problem; design project implementation tools; and manage, monitor and evaluate such projects during their life circle is fundamental in any meaningful approach to the attainment of aid effectiveness.

The case studies reveal an apparent absence of "ownership". Add to this the limited resources, financial as well as manpower, for effective participation in a project and an outcome in terms of low sustainability can be easily predicted. When provincial and district offices lack basic means such as transport and enough personnel to carry out their tasks, the effect will be marginalisation and frustration. Behind these shortcomings lies not only a lack of human resources, put perhaps primarily a lack of financial resources needed to perform the basic functions of the administration. Financially the Zambian economy is in the doldrums. It has been sliding since the mid-70s and in spite of, or perhaps as a result of, structural adjustment it is difficult to see the end of the recession tunnel. The pressure on the GRZ budget is enormous. Almost all government functions are limping, starved of even the most basic resources to conduct their tasks. The effect on aid effectiveness cannot be overstated.

The macroeconomic development of Zambia has been dramatic and discouraging. The country is as close to aid dependency as is possible. External resource transfers will continue to be needed in the foreseeable future. Although, for example, the historically huge fiscal gap has been substantially reduced, this has not really provided any new resources for the government. The structure of the economy has so far not been able to generate needed resources. Structural adjustment has been a "house-cleaning" exercise primarily concerned with establishing a balance in major macroeconomic aggregates, as well as a sound policy framework. The forms of aid have changed over the years, largely reflecting Zambia's success in complying with donor conditionalities, and traditional project support has given way to programme aid in the form of balance of payments support. Balance of payments support, and partly also debt forgiveness, within a framework of structural adjustment policies, is today a dominant feature in aid to Zambia. But how effective is BOP in contributing to growth and development in Zambia?

Recent research into the aid effectiveness of BOP suggests that a major part of these flows has been used for interest payments and amortisations on the international debt. Limited amounts have remained to strengthen Zambia's import capacity. In fact, imports have shown a declining trend since the end of the 1980s, although in a scenario of no-aid, imports would probably have been even lower. This situation highlights the burden of Zambia's indebtedness. It is a major factor reducing the effectiveness of aid. Aid which could have been productively used in the country is now being used for honouring the debt. Given the fact that Zambia's economy is not able, primarily for structural reasons, to generate its own resources at a sufficient level, the national funds released for development purposes remain insufficient for having any particular effect on growth and development.

The existence of the debt overhang is therefore a major constraint to aid effectiveness. As it is today BOP can best be described as a rescheduling of aid inflows. Aid is primarily being used to repay money owed to largely the same countries and institutions that are providing the aid.

What the above conclusions from the Zambian study boil down to is the realisation that the government is currently ill equipped to provide the policy and implementation guidance to the donors so that the latter operate within, and in accordance with, the stipulated national priorities. This incapacity has been aggravated during recent years where government policy in a number of strategic areas has not been clearly and coherently defined, articulated and sustained. However, the lack of policy response from the government cannot be explained only by reference to internal constraints.

During over 10 years of donor relationships Zambia has seen its capacity for independent policy and strategy formulation being severely curtailed. Aid dependency is not restricted to the economic sphere only. The country's dependence on donor policy conditionalities is equally strong.

In a situation where the government has not facilitated a well-functioning framework that allows for effective donor–recipient coordination, donor-driven initiatives, that are not always synchronised with those of the government, have often supplanted the country's vision of development. Donors' priorities (which sometimes conflict with each other) are easily transformed into the recipient's priorities particularly when the government capacity to independently define such priorities has been weakened by organisational and resource constraints. Under such conditions, donors have often been allowed to have an exaggerated latitude to set their own standards and operational procedures that have not always conformed to government expectations.

CHANGING THE AID RELATIONSHIP IN THE FUTURE

In the Zambian case it is very difficult to establish a connection between aid and growth. In spite of structural adjustment policies, there is no supply response forthcoming. This suggests that the basic problem of the Zambian economy is that of structural change, rather than structural adjustment. The issue is if aid can continue to play a progressive role in the future development of Zambia, or if the simple truth is that:

> ... most poor people in most poor countries most of the time never receive or even make contact with aid in any tangible shape or form: whether it is present or absent, increased or decreased, are thus issues that are simply irrelevant to the ways in which they conduct their daily lives. After the multi-billion dollar 'financial flows' involved have been shaken through the sieve of overpriced and irrelevant goods that must be bought in the donor countries, filtered again in the deep pockets of hundreds of thousands of foreign experts and aid agency staff, skimmed off by dishonest commission agents, and stolen by corrupt Ministers and Presidents, there is really very little left to go around.[112]

However, to attribute individual self-interest as their exclusive motive to politicians in developing countries is to deny their sincerity, their merit and, ultimately, their legitimate right to govern.[113]

What happens in the aid interface is in essence a political process. Ideally what should happen is a process where interest groups (stakeholders) exert pressures to maximise their benefit—in terms of power and resources. There is a competitive process between various interest groups. The need to achieve a broad consensus for a government—donor project would require

---

112 Hancock, G, 1996, p. 190.

113 Mosley, P., J. Harrigan & J. Toye, 1991, p. 13.

compromises, where the expectations of the minority would be respected in the process of coalition building. This is how the political competition of interest groups not only protects, but also constructs the public interest. But this is not the process we have seen in the aid relationship in Zambia.

Compromises and coalition building presuppose a constructive dialogue between interest groups. This rarely takes place. Important interest groups on the Zambian side are either not participating in the aid relationship, or are marginalised to the point of being withdrawn or suppressed. The aid relationship is not very competitive. It does not function very well as an arena for communication—or to paraphrase Long—a battlefield for knowledge. The question which quickly emerges is whether it is possible to restore the aid relationship to what it should be. Or whether aid creates inherent power configurations which are difficult to change without questioning the phenomenon of aid as such.

It is always difficult to generalise from a country case such as Zambia. The situation of the country, politically, economically and socially, is such that it is not representative for the developing countries as a whole. There are, however, a group of countries with similar problems—Tanzania, Guinea-Bissau, Mozambique, Angola—to mention some of them. The experiences from the aid relationship in Zambia may well also be found in these countries.

Since the early days of aid it has always been held that for aid to have a potential positive impact it is necessary for certain basic pre-conditions to be present in the host country. There has to be a certain stability (absence of civil war, existence of law and order); there has to be a legal framework, judicial system and institutional structures enabling the government and the economy to function; there has to be a minimum skills level and an administrative structure which enables the state and business to perform its basic functions.[114] One should perhaps also add that what is required is a certain minimum of local resources—manpower, equipment, administration—to put into the aid project, not only during implementation, but perhaps more importantly to ensure sustainability. Much, the same conditions are also important for enabling the government of the host country to participate in the aid relationship in a constructive way. The absence of these conditions does not only have a negative impact on aid effectiveness, but also on the political support for aid in donor and host countries alike. Stokke mentions, in particular, failure to reach the humanitarian and developmental objectives of aid; disrespect of human rights, and; lack of accountability, as particularly influential in eroding support for aid as an institution.[115]

In Zambia, and in any of the other countries mentioned, the basic capacities for receiving aid in an effective way—resources, effective institutions

[114] Riddell, R.C., 1996, pp. 102–103.
[115] Stokke, O. (ed.), 1966, p. 109.

and competence—are not very well represented. It would be tempting to suggest that under such circumstances there are small prospects for restoring the aid relationship and realising the potential impact of aid. Is such a pessimistic scenario really justified? Is the obvious conclusion that aid to countries such as Zambia should be abandoned altogether? We do not think so. But continued aid to Zambia would require a rethinking of the aid strategy and in particular seriously and critically addressing the present imbalances of the aid relationship.

Any attempt to rethink aid would need to have its point of departure in the observed shortcomings of the system of aid, and the aid relationship in particular. The system as it exists today no doubt contains important "systemic flaws". First, aid as an institution is not owned by anyone, consequently no one really feels responsible. Second, in many developing countries leaders are more concerned about the relationship with the donors than their own people. Finally, the actors in the aid arena tend to seek security in clientelistic and cartelistic arrangements.[116]

What would be required then to address these flaws in terms of concrete reform measures? The Zambian experience would suggest the following measures to be undertaken:

— The interface of the aid relationship has to be opened up allowing other local stakeholders to participate. Today it is dominated by government officials, politicians and businessmen who all have distinct interests in the resources provided by foreign aid. It is rare to see provincial and/or district officers, not to mention the supposed beneficiaries of aid in the villages and urban centres, involved in the design, appraisal and implementation of a project. Needless to say such a reform will have substantial implications for how aid is organised and managed by the donor and by the host country.

— The level of aid flows should be determined according to what the host country can realistically accommodate. Thus, it is important to distinguish between actual needs and actual capacity to receive aid.

— Linked to this is an upgrading of the concept of sustainability. Traditionally it assumes some significance only at the point of evaluating an aid project. It has a much more marginal role to play at the stage of appraisal and project design. Rarely do project designers reflect on what is required by the local parties to "take over" the project, in terms of resources, once the actual aid assistance has been terminated.

— The strong negative impact on the aid relationship and aid effectiveness exercised by a resource starved government has implications for

116 Hydén, G., 1996, p. 198.

the current insufficient aid coordination that takes place. Coordination is required primarily to make more efficient use of limited government resources. The case of Zambia clearly shows the need for a move from the current dominant donor-driven aid coordination, to a mode of coordination with its origin in national planning and policy making.

— Donors have to subordinate themselves to existing local administrative structures and procedures. In countries like Zambia it is tempting to bypass such structures, or force them to adapt to procedures which are preferred by donors. The consequences are sometimes dramatic. Overburdened officials are left with the task of manoeuvring between the requirements of their own systems and those of a multiplicity of donors.

— Conditionalities in their present form need to be revised. Conditions which effectively mean a substantial involvement in national affairs, do not contribute to an effective aid relationship, nor to aid effectiveness. In the short term they may yield some results, but the long-term effects are counterproductive to the intended purpose. They tend to perpetuate a relation characterised by dominance, rather than opening up for a dialogue between "equal" partners.

The outcome of all these reform measures is an aid system which takes its point of departure from a host country perspective. Local conditions and capacities should become the starting point for any aid programme, rather than a "contextual footnote".[117] The operational implications of seriously applying such a perspective are, however, far-reaching. The organisation and management of aid will need to be changed, if local level stakeholders shall be integrated in the decision-making process. The "disbursement" target will be difficult to achieve, if local capacities to receive shall determine the actual level of aid flows. Projects and programmes will take longer time to plan and implement.

The "aid industry" does not really lack a debate on what is good development aid, the best practices etc. Every year the aid agencies themselves, NGOs, various research institutes produce an impressive amount of studies and reports on aid policies. Equally abundant are analyses on aid performance and what determines effective aid.[118] The authors of this study have,

---

[117] Bossuyt, J. & G. Laporte, 1995.

[118] A sample of such texts could include the following:
OECD, *Participatory Development and Good Governance*. Paris: DAC, 1995;
OECD, *Development Partnership in the New Global Context*. Paris: SG/Press, 1995;
The Netherlands Ministry of Foreign Affairs, *A World of Difference: A New Framework for Development Cooperation in the 1990s*. The Hague: Ministry of Foreign Affairs, 1993;
World Bank, *The World Bank and the Poorest Countries. Support for Development in the 1990s*. Washington D.C.: World Bank 1994;
World Bank, *Effective Implementation: Key to Development Impact. Report from the Portfolio Management Task Force*. Washington D.C.: World Bank, 1992;

over the years, read a number of them. Without having done any scientific text analyses of these documents, we feel that there are some typical traits in all of them which raise some reservations as to the possibility to actually reform the basic principles for foreign aid.

First, almost all policy related studies accept the basic assumption that aid is necessary and has a natural role to play in the development of the Third World. The early critics of aid, for example Peter Bauer and Keith Griffin, seems to be forgotten. One would have thought that after 25–30 years of experience from development aid it would be appropriate to approach the issue of the relevance of aid in a more open manner.

This leads us then to our second observation. There is a discrepancy between what is being proposed as good policies, best practices etc. and actual operations in the field. Independent analysts, and sometimes even those responsible for policy formulation in the aid agencies, may stress the importance of a "recipient perspective" and ensuring the commitment of the host government. However, when examining actual practice there is little to be seen. Donors continue to push for their own development agenda, enforce strict appraisal and monitoring procedures, as well as measures to control implementation.

Third, analyses of the determinants of success and failures rarely come down to discussing the influence of various stakeholder interests on the interaction in the aid relationship. The findings of this study are probably not unique. Everybody with some experience from development aid doubtless recognises much of what we have revealed in our case studies. The more interesting thing is the failure of aid to take any decisive action to rectify this situation. The unwillingness to address the real issues of power and interests, results in policy prescriptions of a type exemplified in the following quotation:

> Donors had often acted as if development could be initiated and managed from outside, possibly in alliance with one powerful minister or with a small segment of the bureaucratic elite. A shift in donor attitudes is now required, in response to the process of democratisation they themselves have supported. The transformation by donors, from seeing themselves as determining policy to a genuine joint partnership in a new dialogue with recipients of aid may require a profound attitudinal change. For a new dialogue, donors must be willing to take recipients' decisions, strategies and approaches to implementation more seriously. The concept of national ownership of projects and programmes deserves more than the lip service it currently receives.[119]

The problem with these kinds of policy proposals are not that they are wrong. On the contrary, it is not difficult to agree with them. A change is certainly required, but the question is whether change is at all possible. This

---

SIDA, *State, Market and Aid: Redefined Roles.* Stockholm: SIDA, 1994; and
Berg, E., et al., *Rethinking Technical Cooperation. Reforms for Capacity Building in Africa.* New York: UNDP, 1993.

119 Havnevik, K. & van B. Arkadie, 1996, p. 21.

can only be answered by conducting a thorough analysis of what drives donors, or the host country representatives for that matter, to act the way they do. Without such an understanding of what makes the parties in the aid relationship tick, it is difficult to devise policies and strategies that can be effectively translated into good practices.

Bibliographic References

Adam, C. et al., *Evaluation of Swedish Development Cooperation with Zambia.* Stockholm: SASDA, 1994.

Adams, S. "The Structure and Dynamics of Behavior in Organizational Boundary Roles", in M. Dunette, *Handbook of Industrial and Organizational Psychology.* Chicago: Rand McNally, 1976.

Adamson, A., "Institutional Framework for Planning, Co-ordinating and Monitoring of Development in the Districts and Provinces", *Cabinet Circular* No. 1/1995, 3 January 1995.

Andersson, P. & S. Kayizzi-Mugerwa, *External Shocks and the Search for Diversification in Zambia.* Mimeo. Department of Economics. University of Gothenburg, 1994.

Andersson, P. & M. Ndulo, *Hyperinflation, Stabilisation, and the New Economic Recovery Program,* Mimeo. Department of Economics. University of Gothenburg, 1994.

Andersson, P. & M. Ndulo, *Structural Adjustment, Inflation and Political Commitment in Zambia: A Short Analysis of the New Economic Programme of 1989.* Macroeconomic Studies 28/92. Stockholm: SIDA, 1992.

Arce, A. & N. Long, "The Dynamics of Knowledge. Interfaces Between Bureaucrats and Peasants", in N. Long & A. Long, *Battlefields of Knowledge. The Interlocking of Theory and Practice in Social Research and Development.* London: Routledge, 1992

Bauer, P.T., *Equality, the Third World and Economic Delusion.* London: Methuen, 1992.

Berg, E., *Rethinking Technical Cooperation. Reforms for Capacity Building in Africa.* New York: UNDP, 1993.

Bigsten, A. et al., *Evaluation of Swedish Development Cooperation with Zambia.* SASDA. Ds 1994:114.

Blase, M., *Institution Building: A Source Book.* East Lansing, Michigan: Midwest Universities Consortium for International Activities, Inc., 1973.

Bossuyt, J. & G. Laporte, *Partnership in the 1990's: How to Make it Work Better.* Policy Management Brief no 3, 1995. Maastricht: European Centre for Development Policy Management.

Brown, D.L., *Managing Conflict at Organizational Interfaces.* Reading, Massachusetts: Addison-Wesley Publishing Company, 1983.

Cassen, R., et al., *Does Aid Work?* Oxford: Clarendon Press, 1989

Carlsson, J., G. Köhlin & A. Ekbom, *The Political Economy of Evaluation. International Aid Agencies and the Effectiveness of Aid.* London: Macmillan, 1994.

Coase, R., "The Problem of Social Cost", *Journal of Law and Economics,* 3(1):1–44, 1960.

DWA/CCMU (Department of Water Affairs/Community Management and Monitoring Unit) , *Preliminary Analysis of the Water Point Inventory in Eastern, Southern and Central Provinces.* Lusaka: CMMU, 1994.

DWA/NORAD (Department of Water Affairs /Norwegian Agency for International Development), *Water Supply and Sanitation Programme: Western Province. Proposed NORAD support in the period 1994–96.* Mongu: Provincial Water Engineer/RB Consultants Int. A/S, February 1994.

Economist Intelligence Unit, *Country Reports and Country Profiles for Zambia.* London: EIU, 1993.

Engberg-Pedersen, P., "The Politics of Good Development Aid: Behind the Clash of Aid Rationales", in K. Havnevik & B. van Arkadie (eds.), *Domination or Dialogue? Experiences and Prospects for African Development Cooperation.* Uppsala: Nordic Africa Institute, 1996.

Fergus, M. et al., *Evaluation of the Water Supply Programme in Western Province, Zambia*. Lusaka, 1987.

Forss, K., O. Saasa & J. Carlsson, *A Study of Coordination in the Zambian Education Sector. With a Focus on International Development Cooperation*. Stockholm: SIDA, January 1995.

Garaway, G., "The Case Study Model: An Organizational Strategy for Cross-Cultural Evaluation", *Evaluation*, Vol. 2 No. 2, 1966.

Glaser, B. & A.L. Strauss, *The Discovery of Grounded Theory*. New York: Aldine Publishers, 1967.

GRZ (Government of the Republic of Zambia), *Adjustment in Africa: The Zambian experience*. Paper Presented by the Ministry of Finance/Bank of Zambia to the World Bank Seminar on Adjustment in Africa, Harare, 1994.

GRZ/NORAD (Government of the Republic of Zambia/Norwegian Agency for International Development), *Agreed Minutes of the Fourth Annual Meeting, Water Supply Programme: Western Province*. Mongu, April 1994.

GRZ (Government of the Republic of Zambia), *Budget Address*, various years.

GRZ (Government of the Republic of Zambia), *Economic Review*. Lusaka: NCDP, 1992.

GRZ (Government of the Republic of Zambia), *Economic Review*. January–June 1993. Lusaka: NCDP, 1993.

GRZ (Government of the Republic of Zambia), *Focus on Learning*. Lusaka, 1992.

GRZ (Government of the Republic of Zambia), *Monthly Digest of Statistics*, various issues.

Gulhati, R., *Impasse in Zambia: The Economics and Politics of Reform*. Development Policy Case Series No. 2. Economic Development Institute, Washington: World Bank, 1989.

Gummesson, E.M., *Qualitative Methods in Management Research*. Lund: Studentlitteratur/Chartwell-Bratt, 1988.

Hancock, G., *Lords of Poverty*. London: Mandarin Books, 1996.

Havnevik, K., & B. van Arkadie (eds.), *Domination or Dialogue? Experiences and Prospects for African Development Cooperation*. Uppsala: Nordic Africa Institute, 1996.

Hayter, T., *Aid as Imperialism*. Harmondsworth: Penguin, 1971.

Hydén, G., "From Bargaining to Marketing: How to Reform Foreign Aid in the 1990s", in O. Stokke (ed.), *Foreign Aid towards the Year 2000: Experiences and Challenges*. EADI Book Series 18. London: Frank Cass, 1966.

IMF (International Monetary Fund), *Government Finance Statistics*, various years.

JICA (Japanese International Cooperation Agency), *Basic Design Study Report on Groundwater Development Project (Phase II) in Southern Province in the Republic of Zambia*. Tokyo: JICA, 1988.

JICA (Japanese International Cooperation Agency), "Japan's Grant Aid Supervised by Ministry of Foreign Affairs/JICA", *The International Development Journal*. Tokyo, 1986.

Katz, D. & R.L. Kahn. *The Social Psychology of Organizations* (2nd ed.). New York: Wiley, 1978.

Kelly, M. J., P. Stoije, B. Lindahl, J.Z. Banda, & E.N. Phiri, *Zambia Educational Materials Project (ZEMP): Evaluation of Phase II*. Lusaka: Ministry of Education, 1991.

Knorr-Cetina, K.D., *The Manufacture of Knowledge: An Essay on the Constructivist and Contextual Nature of Science*. Oxford: Pergamon Press, 1981.

Korten, D. & F. Alfonso (eds.), *Bureaucracy and the Poor: Closing the Gap*. Singapore: McGraw Hill, 1981.

Kruger, A. et al., *Water Supply and Sanitation Programme: Western Province. A Project Review for NORAD and GRZ*. Lusaka, November 1992.

Larsson, K., *Strukturanpassning. Bistånd och utveckling*. Stockholm: SIDA, 1994.

Lipton, M. & J. Toye, *Does Aid Work in India?* London: Routledge, 1991.

Long, N., *Encounters at the Interface: A Perspective on Social Discontinuities in Rural Development*. Wageningen Studies in Sociology 27. Wageningen: The Agricultural University, 1989.

Moore, M., *Institution Building as a Development Assistance Method*. SIDA Evaluation Report 1995/1. Stockholm: SIDA, 1995.

Mosley, P., *Overseas Aid: Its Defence and Reform*. Brighton: Wheatsheaf, 1987.

Mosley, P., J. Harrigan & J. Toye, *Aid and Power. The World Bank and Policy-Based lending*. London: Routledge, 1991.

Mwanawima, I. & H. White, *Swedish Balance of Payments Support to Zambia*. Final report. SIDA, February 1995.

The Netherlands Ministry of Foreign Affairs, *A World of Difference: A New Framework for Development Cooperation in the 1990s*. The Hague: Ministry of Foreign Affairs, 1993.

Normann, R. A., *Personal Quest for Methodology*. Stockholm: Scandinavian Institute for Administrative Research, 1970.

North, D., "Economic Performance through Time", *The American Economic Review*, Vol. 84 No. 3, pp. 359–368.

North, D., *Institutions, Institutional Change and Economic Performance*. New York: Cambridge University Press, 1990.

OECD (Organisation of Economic Cooperation and Development), *Development Partnership in the New Global Context*. Paris: SG/Press, 1995.

OECD (Organisation of Economic Cooperation and Development), *Geographical Distribution of Financial Flows to Developing Countries*, various issue.

OECD (Organisation of Economic Cooperation and Development), *Participatory Development and Good Governance*. Paris: DAC, 1995.

Pacific Consultants International, *Completion Report for the Project for the Groundwater Development in Southern Province*. Vol. 1. Tokyo: JICA, 1990.

Riddell, R.C., *Foreign Aid Reconsidered*. Baltimore: John Hopkins University Press/Overseas Development Institute, 1987.

Riddell, R.C., "Major Issues Related to the New Framework for International Development Cooperation", in K. Havnevik & B. van Arkadie (eds.), *Domination or Dialogue? Experiences and Prospects for African Development Cooperation*. Uppsala: Nordic Africa Institute, 1996.

Rondinelli, D.A., *Development Projects as Policy Experiments. An Adaptive Approach to Development Administration*. London: Routledge, 1990.

Rundin, U. et al., *Evaluation of Swedish Support to the Drought Operations in Southern Africa*. Stockholm: SIDA, 1993.

Saasa, O., *Evaluation of Zambia's Attitudes, Policies and Procedures Concerning Technical Assistance Personnel*. Stockholm: SIDA, September 1987.

Saasa, O., "Structural Adjustment and Governance Capacity in Zambia, 1983–1994". Report presented to the Governance and Successful Adjustment Conference, November 9–11. Washington: World Bank, 1994.

SADCC (Southern African Development Coordination Conference), *Drought Emergency in Southern Africa (DESA)*. DHA/93/71. Geneva, 1993.

Schein, E., *Organizational Psychology* (2nd ed.). Englewood Cliffs, NJ: Prentice Hall, 1970.

Sedin, B & S. Lööf, *Southern Africa Drought Relief Transport*. Stockholm: SIDA, 1992.

Selznick, P., *Leadership in Administration*. New York: Harper and Row, 1957.

Seppala, J., (Distribution Adviser), *Final Report*. Lusaka: Ministry of Education, 1992.

Simon, H., "Rationality in Psychology and Economics", in R.M. Hogerth & M.L. Reder (eds.), *Rational Choice*. Chicago and London: The University of Chicago Press, 1986.

Stokke, O. (ed.), *Foreign Aid towards the Year 2000: Experiences and Challenges*. EADI Book Series 18. London: Frank Cass, 1966.

Svedberg, P., A. Olofsgård & B. Ekman, *Evaluation of Swedish Development Co-operation with Guinea-Bissau*. Ministry of Foreign Affairs, Ds 1994:77.

Thomas, J.M. & W.G. Bennis, *Management of Change and Conflict*. Harmondsworth: Penguin, 1972.

Times of Zambia. 26 September 1994. Lusaka.

UNDP (United Nations Development Programme), *Development Cooperation: Zambia 1991*. Lusaka: UNDP, 1992.

UNDP (United Nations Development Programme), *Development Cooperation: Zambia, 1991*. Lusaka: UNDP, 1993.

UNDP (United Nations Development Programme), *Development Cooperation: Zambia 1992*. Lusaka: UNDP, 1995.

UNDP (United Nations Development Programme), *Restructuring and Development in Zambia: Roles for Technical Cooperation*. New York: UNDP, 1986.

Wai, D., *The Sustainability of ACBF Funded Projects*. Harare: African Capacity Building Foundation, 1994.

White, H. & T. Edstrand, "Aid Impact in Debt Stressed Economy: The Case of Zambia", in H. White et al., *The Macroeconomics of Aid: Case Studies of Four Countries*. Stockholm: SASDA, 1994.

White, H. & J. Luttik, *The Countrywide Effects of Aid. Policy research working paper 1337*. Washington: World Bank, August 1994.

White, H., et al., *The Macroeconomics of Aid: Case Studies of Four Countries*. Stockholm: SASDA, 1994.

World Bank, *Adjustment in Africa. Reforms, Results and the Road Ahead*. Washington: World Bank/Oxford University Press, 1994.

World Bank, *Effective Implementation: Key to Development Impact. Report from the Portfolio Management Task Force*. Washington D.C.: World Bank.

World Bank, *Engendering Sustainable Growth in Zambia: A Gender Strategy for Promoting Economic Effectiveness*. Washington D.C.: World Bank, Population and Human Resources Division, Southern Africa Department, 1994.

World Bank, *The World Bank and the Poorest Countries. Support for Development in the 1990s*. Washington D.C.: World Bank.

World Bank, *Zambia: Prospects for Sustainable and Equitable Growth*. Washington D.C.: World Bank, 1993.

Yin, R.K., *Case Study Research. Design and Methods*. Newburg Park, CA: Sage, 1991.

ZEMP (Zambia Educational Materials Project), *Quarterly Report. October–December 1993*. Lusaka.

ZEMP, *Quarterly Report, January–March 1993*. Lusaka, 1995.

ZEMP (Zambia Educational Materials Project), *Quarterly Report. January–March 1994*. Lusaka, 1994.

The Aid Relationship in Zambia
A Conflict Scenario

by

Oliver Saasa & Jerker Carlsson

The Institute for African Studies, Lusaka, Zambia
and
The Nordic Africa Institute, Uppsala, Sweden

Professor **Oliver Saasa** is Director of the Institute for African Studies at the University of Zambia. He has also worked extensively as a consultant to many international aid agencies.

Jerker Carlsson leads the research program on "Aid Effectiveness in Africa" at the Nordic Africa Institute. He is also adjunct Professor at the Department of Peace- and Development Research (PADRIGU), University of Gothenburg, where he is running a research school on aid evaluation.

Indexing terms
Development aid
Aid evaluation
Development projects
Aid cooperation
Zambia

The opinions expressed in this volume are those of the authors and do not necessarily reflect the views of Nordiska Afrikainstitutet.

Cover illustration: The *Kuomboka ceremony* of the Lozi people.
The *Litunga's* great barge is rowed out of Lealui at dawn.
Water colour painting by Kim Forss.

Language checking: Elaine Almén

ISBN 91-7106-399-4

Printed in Sweden by
Gotab, Stockholm 1996